SOUL EATER NOT!

5

ATSUSHI OHKUBO

EATER

ATSUSHI
OHKUBO

T!

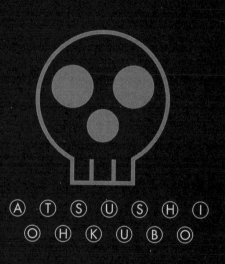

SOUL

05

NO

SOUL EATER NOT!

05

CONTENTS

SOUL EATER NOT!
ETERNAL DARKNESS

SOUL EATER NOT!

ARE WE REALLY GOING TO DO THIS?
YOU GOTTA HAVE BAIT TO GO FISHING.
IT DOESN'T FEEL RIGHT TO ME...
WE CAN'T USE HER AS BAIT TO DRAW OUT SHAULA...
THE DEATH FESTIVAL IS TO-MORROW.
WE CAN'T SIT UP ON OUR HIGH HORSE AND WATCH.
TOMB
WE HAVE TO FOLLOW UP ON THIS VALUABLE LEAD AND CORNER SHAULA.
STUB-BORN—THAT'S THE KIND OF MAN I AM.

GU
(SQUEEZE)

SOUL EATER NOT!

CHAPTER 26: ETERNAL DARKNESS

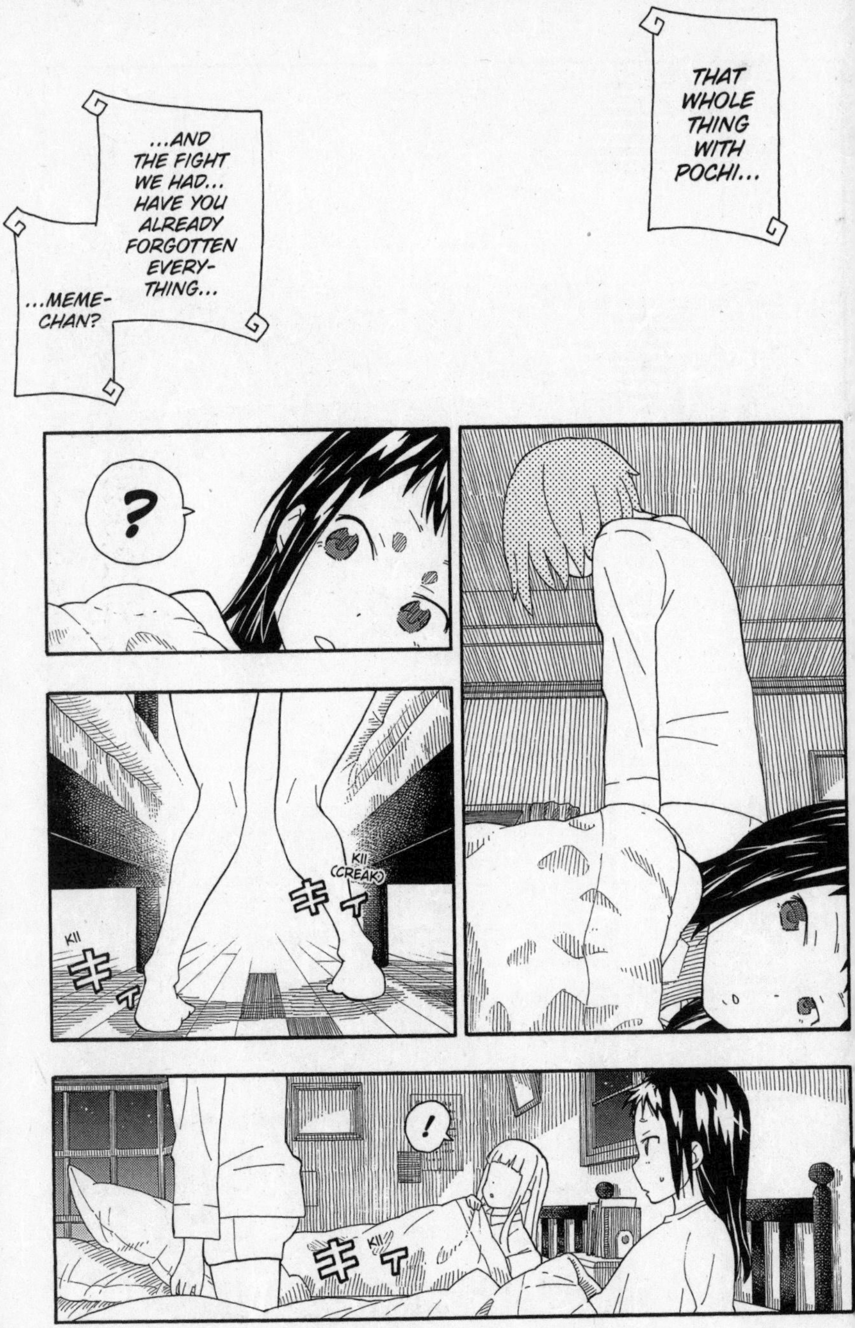
THAT WHOLE THING WITH POCHI...
...AND THE FIGHT WE HAD... HAVE YOU ALREADY FORGOTTEN EVERY-THING...
...MEME-CHAN?
?
KII (CREAK)
キィ
KII
キィ
!
KII
キィ

...
...
THAT'S... HER HALLOWEEN COSTUME, ISN'T IT? WHERE IS SHE GOING ...?
MAYBE WE SHOULD WAKE HER UP AND TAKE HER BACK HOME...
I'VE NEVER SEEN SOMEONE SLEEP SO REST-LESSLY...
THAT DOESN'T COUNT AS SLEEP-ING...

SFX: WAKU (GIDDY) WAKU
NO.
I MUST OBSERVE WHAT SHE DOES AND REPORT MY FINDINGS TO HER LATER.
YOU CAN WAIT BACK IN THE DORM ROOM, TSUGUMI-SAN.
...
WELL, I DON'T THINK I CAN GO BACK TO SLEEP ANY-WAY, SO...
Augustiner-Brau
Goldener Engl
FURA (SLUMP)
JUST HOW FAR IS SHE GOING TO WALK...?
NOT

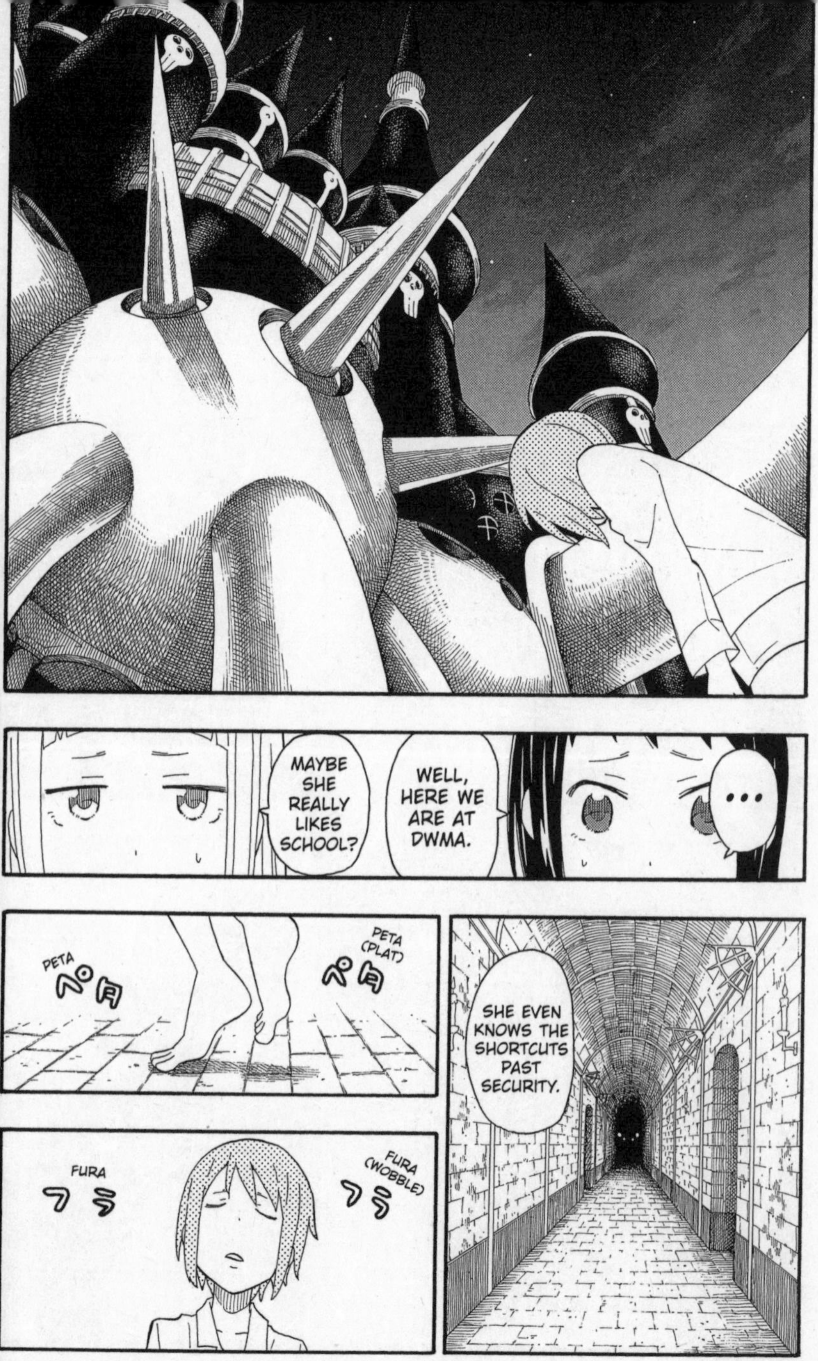
...
WELL, HERE WE ARE AT DWMA.
MAYBE SHE REALLY LIKES SCHOOL?
SHE EVEN KNOWS THE SHORTCUTS PAST SECURITY.
ペタ
PETA (PLAT)
ペタ
PETA
フラ
FURA (WOBBLE)
フラ
FURA

ANTI-WITCH HEADQUARTERS

FOR WITCH
...
IT'S THE ANTI-WITCH HQ...
MAYBE SHE'S DREAMING OF WHEN WE VISITED HERE BEFORE?
NOT
CHARI (JINGLE)
チャリ...
KACHA (CLICK)
カチャ
WHY DOES MEME-CHAN HAVE THE KEY?
SHE'S NOT ALLOWED IN THERE!
LET'S GO.
...

GASA (RUSTLE)
GASA
PERA (FLIP)
MEME-SAN, WHAT ARE YOU DOING!?
YOU CAN'T BE IN HERE!
!
!
WHAT ARE YOU DOING HERE AT THIS TIME OF NIGHT?
TORON (DAZE)

SU (SSSK)
DOSHA (THWUMP)
MEME-CHAN!!
ARE YOU ALL RIGHT!?
...
IS THIS...A HALLOW-EEN COSTUME ...?
MEME-SAN? MEME-SAN?

PRIN-CESS! GET AWAY FROM THERE!!
!!
DOSU (WHUMP)
ZUN (KRRSH)

MEME ... CHAN ...
NOT
DA (LEAP)
DOGA (BWOOM)
AAGH!!
BASA (FLAP)

I'M GOING AFTER TATANE !!
STAY HERE WITH THEM, CLAY!!
NO, I'LL GO WITH YOU!!
...
...I GUESS WE CAN'T LEAVE THEM ALONE...
BA (WHOOSH)
TATANE'S ON THE RUN, SID-SENSEI. SHE'S HEADING FOR THE FRONT ENTRANCE.

YOU'RE NOT HURT, ARE YOU...?
CLAY-SAN!! WHAT'S HAPPENED TO MEME-SAN!? WHAT'S GOING ON!?
I'LL EXPLAIN, BUT YOU HAVE TO REMAIN CALM...
I'M AT THE FRONT GATE.
TARGET'S ON HER WAY.
SNIPER TEAM, YOU READY?
READY WHENEVER YOU ARE—

!!
トス
TOSU (THUK)
ジャラ
JARA (JANGLE)
PIRI (FFT)
ピリ
PIRI
ピリ
PIRI
ピリ
PIRI
ピリ

SO...
...YOU'RE TELLING US MEME-SAN IS WORKING WITH THE WITCHES!?
DON'T PANIC ...
WE'RE ALMOST POSITIVE THAT TATANE DID STEAL THE INFORMATION.
WE'LL HAVE CONCRETE PROOF SOON ENOUGH.
THAT'S A LIE!
......IT CAN'T BE...
MY BELIEF IS...
...THAT TATANE IS BEING CONTROLLED BY THE WITCHES.
......HUH!?
WHAT DO YOU MEAN?
I THINK THE VARIOUS ABNORMAL "TRAITOR" INCIDENTS AND THE ATTACK ON ETERNAL FEATHER ARE THE WORK OF THE SAME WITCH...
TA (TEKO)
TA

SHAULA GORGON.
TON (TAP)
ITY
SOME KIND OF HYPNOTIC MENTAL CONTROL THROUGH A FOREIGN TOXIN...
THEN MEME-SAN'S JUST A VICTIM!
BUT THERE'S SOMETHING UNIQUE ABOUT TATANE'S CASE.
UNLIKE THE OTHER TRAITORS, SHE HASN'T BEEN SUFFERING FROM INSOMNIA OR LOSS OF EMOTION...
BASED ON HER SIDE EFFECTS—LIKE HER ACTIONS TONIGHT AND HER TYPICAL MEMORY LOSS—I SUSPECT SHE'S UNDER A MUCH HIGHER FORM OF MIND CONTROL...
HUH?
LOSS OF MEMO-RY?
SIDE EFFECTS ...?

BUT WE WON'T KNOW FOR SURE UNTIL WE'VE BROUGHT HER SAFELY INTO OUR CUSTODY.
WHY DO YOU ALWAYS FORGET EVERY-THING?
IT'S AWFUL... YOU FORGET THE SAD THINGS, THE HAPPY THINGS...
YOU EVEN FORGOT WHAT JUST HAP-PENED!
I BET YOU'RE GOING TO FORGET ALL ABOUT ME ONE OF THESE DAYS TOO!!
......I' SORRY
I FORGO SOMETHIN IMPORTAN AGAIN...
ND NOW VE HURT YOU...
I'M SORRY.
SO MEME-CHAN'S FORGET-FULNESS IS BECAUSE OF A WITCH'S HYPNOSIS ...?
I CAN'T BE TOTALLY SURE...
...
I'M HEADING OUT TO KEEP TATANE SAFE.
WE'LL SEND SOME SECURITY TO THE GIRLS' DORM FOR YOU.
JUST WAIT HERE FOR NOW.

TRY NOT TO HURT HER IF AT ALL POSSIBLE... HERE SHE COMES.
!
!
CHUN (TSST)
SNIP-ERS!?
TAN (DSH)
TAN

TAKE COVER!!
SNIPER TEAM! WHAT'S GOING ON!!? COME IN!!
BABA (LEAP)
!!
TAN.
TAN
YOU STAY HERE!
I'LL GO AFTER TATANE!

DA (DASH)
MEME-CHAN...
I'M SO SORRY ...

WHY DO YOU ALWAYS FORGET EVERY-THING?
IT'S AWFUL...YOU FORGET THE SAD THINGS, THE HAPPY THINGS...
YOU EVEN FORGOT WHAT JUST HAPPENED!
I BET YOU'RE GOING TO FORGET ALL ABOUT ME ONE OF THESE DAYS TOO!!
I... I CAN'T BELIEVE IT...
I HAD NO IDEA WHAT WAS HAPPEN-ING TO HER...
...BUT I SAID SUCH AWFUL THINGS...
SU (SHF)

IT'S REALLY TOO BAD ABOUT YOUR LITTLE POCHI-SAN.
THERE'S NOTHING WE CAN DO...
...AND I DON'T THINK MEME-SAN BLAMES YOU FOR ANYTHING.
BUT RIGHT NOW OUR PARTNER IS UNDER A WITCH'S HYPNOSIS, BEING FORCED TO PERFORM EVIL ACTS. HER FREEDOM HAS BEEN STOLEN.
IS IT REALLY TIME FOR YOU TO STAND HERE AND CRY!?

I was told that the common people were strong, hardy, fun, and cheerful folk.
That's why I chose you for my partner, Tsugumi-san.
Are you going to play the obedient type and wait here?
GUJI
KUJI (RUB)

LET'S GO, ANYA-SAN!!
THERE'S NOT MUCH I CAN DO...
...BUT AT LEAST I CAN APOLOGIZE TO MEME-CHAN!!
HYUOOO (WHOOSH)
...

I IMAGINED THINGS WOULD BE IN COMPLETE MAYHEM OUT HERE...
...BUT IT'S STILL VERY QUIET...
EEK!
BASA (FWAP)
PATE
PATE (FLAP)
A BAT?
LOOK AT THAT!!
IT'S WHAT MEME-CHAN ALWAYS USED...
MES-SEN-GER BATS!?
A MES-SEN-GER BAT!?
MES-SENGER BAT?
LET'S FOLLOW IT, ANYA-SAN!!

TA-TANE... CAN YOU HEAR ME?

MEME TATANE... EXCELLENT GRADES...POSSESSES SEVERAL JUNIOR TITLES IN MULTIPLE FIELDS INCLUDING KARATE AND JUDO...
WAS SHE TARGETED BY THE WITCHES BECAUSE OF HER OVERALL SKILL...?
ZA (SKSH)
ZA
ZA
ZA

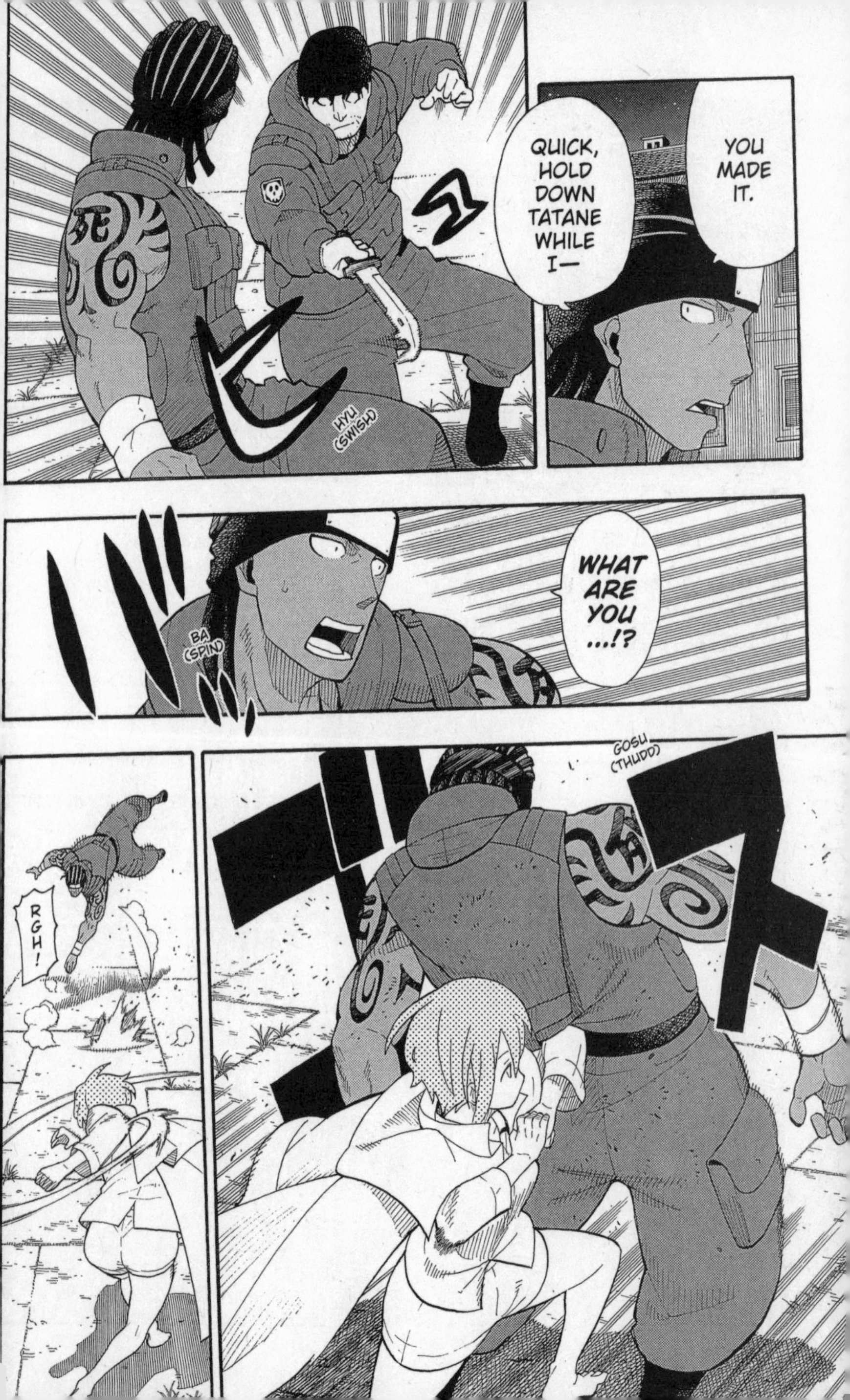
YOU MADE IT.
QUICK, HOLD DOWN TATANE WHILE I—
HYU (SWISH)
WHAT ARE YOU ...!?
BA (SPIN)
GOSU (THUDD)
RGH!

THEY'RE BEING CON- TROLLED BY THE WITCH?
ZAZA (ZSHH)
......
DOSU (SHOONK)

ビク
BIKU
ビク
BIKU
(TWITCH)
DID YOU THINK YOU COULD LURE ME OUT?
WELL, IT SEEMS IT'S YOU WHO FELL INTO THE TRAP.
ピク
PIKU
(TWITCH)
ピク
PIKU
AH...
AHH...
YOU'RE MUCH TOO DANGER-OUS...I DON'T NEED THE MOST TALENTED SERVANTS.
I JUST NEED OBEDIENT SOLDIERS.

ドゴ
DOGON (BOOM)
WHAT WAS THAT SOUND !?
AKA-NE-SAN!?
!
TA (TEK)
TA
TA
... YOU GOTTA BE KID-DING ME...

SOUL EATER NOT!

THE DEATH FEST HAS BEGUN!

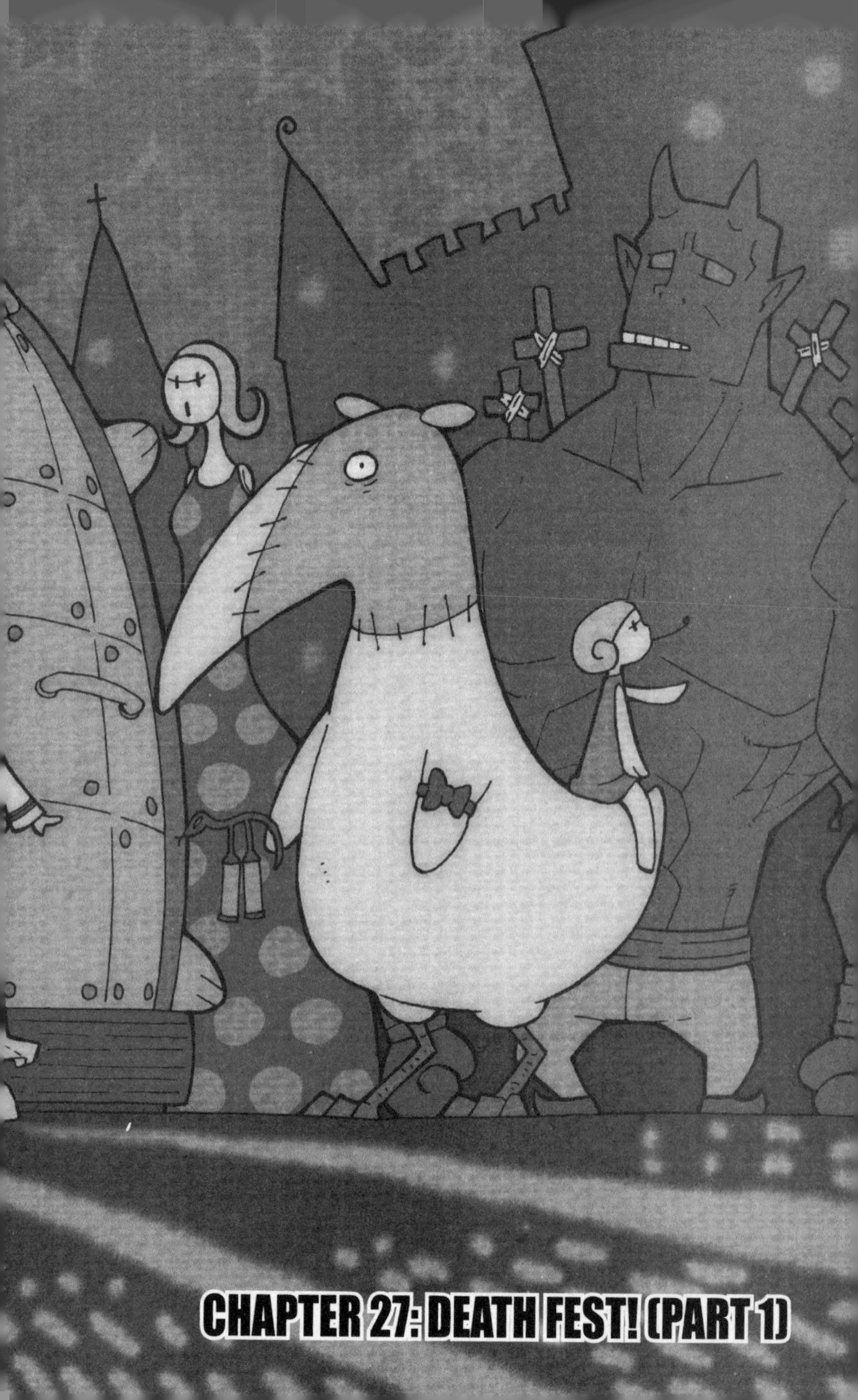

CHAPTER 27: DEATH FEST! (PART 1)

SOUL EATER NOT!

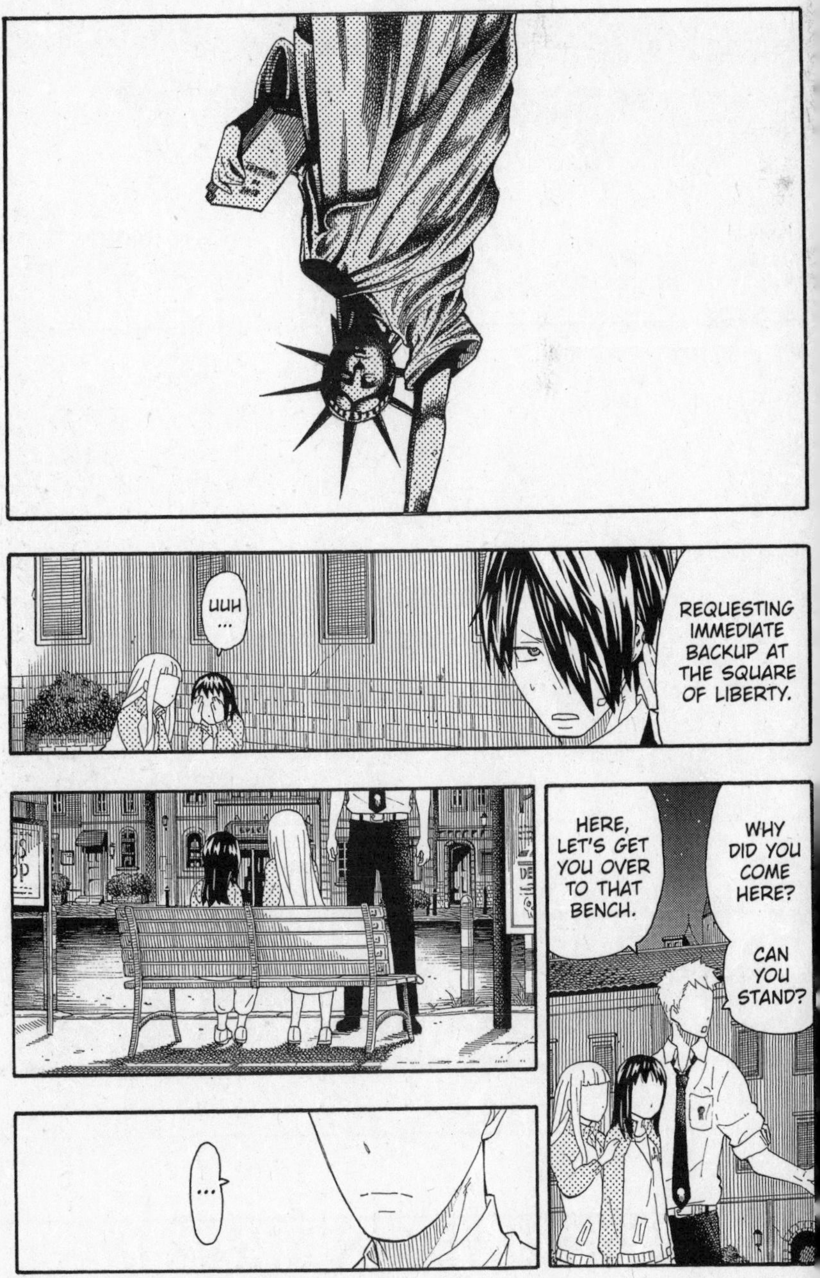
REQUESTING IMMEDIATE BACKUP AT THE SQUARE OF LIBERTY.
UUH ...
WHY DID YOU COME HERE?
CAN YOU STAND?
HERE, LET'S GET YOU OVER TO THAT BENCH.
...

SOUL EATER NOT!

CHAPTER 27: DEATH FEST! (PART 1)

?
PRINCESS... ANASTASIA?
HOW!?
WE HAD AN AGREEMENT WITH YOUR COUNTRY THAT IF YOU SHOULD FALL INTO DANGER, YOU WOULD BE RETURNED HOME AT ONCE.
SID-SENSEI ORDERED US TO MAKE THE CALL IF ANYTHING HAPPENED.
NOT
BUT WHY YOU...?
WE'RE "EAT"-CLASS STUDENTS WORKING WITH THE DWMA-CIA. THE ONLY REASON WE WERE ENROLLED IN THE "NOT"-CLASS WAS TO PROTECT YOU IN SECRET.

FUAN
FUAN (WEE-OO)
I'LL TAKE IT FROM HERE.
THANK YOU.
SU (SHP)
COME ON.
WAIT JUST ONE MINUTE! I CAN'T LEAVE ON MY OWN!
I WILL NOT DESERT MY PART-NERS!
PA (SNATCH)
NOT
YOU AREN'T OFFICIALLY PARTNERS.
EVEN SO, THAT'S—
SID-SENSEI IS DEAD!!

WE CAN'T PLAY GAMES WITH YOU ANY-MORE!
...
I'M SORRY ...
PON (PAT)
WE HAVE A CAR TO TAKE YOU BACK TO DWMA. PLEASE, THIS WAY...

ANYA-SAN!!
WHAT DOES THIS MEAN!?
...

YOU SHOULD RETURN TO YOUR DORM.
ANYA-SAN!!

BANNER: DEATH FESTIVAL

SHIRT: DEATH FESTIVAL

031
死武祭!!
CALENDAR: DEATH FEST!
HOW IS SHE?
NOTHING TO REPORT.
I GET THAT SHE'S UNDER CURFEW, BUT A GUARD SEEMS UNNEC-ESSARY.
YOU CAN'T BLAME THEM... SID-SENSEI WAS KILLED, MEME'S MISS-ING, AND ANYA WENT HOME.
I DON'T KNOW ANY DETAILS. THEY SAID MEME'S ONE OF THE SUSPECTS...?
......
WHAT ABOUT ANYA?
HER ESCORT'S HERE NOW. THEY'RE GOING TO TAKE HER STRAIGHT TO THE AIR-PORT FROM DWMA...

THEY WON'T STOP BY THE DORM.
LET'S BE ON OUR WAY, PRIN-CESS.
!
AH...
THANK YOU, ALFRED.
?

GOT IT? DON'T LET YOUR EMO-TIONS GET THE BEST OF YOU—DON'T LOOK FOR REVENGE.
I'LL BE TAKING COMMAND IN SID'S ABSENCE.
I'M SORRY, BUT...
!
...WE NEED YOUR HELP.
BURORORO (VRRRRRM)

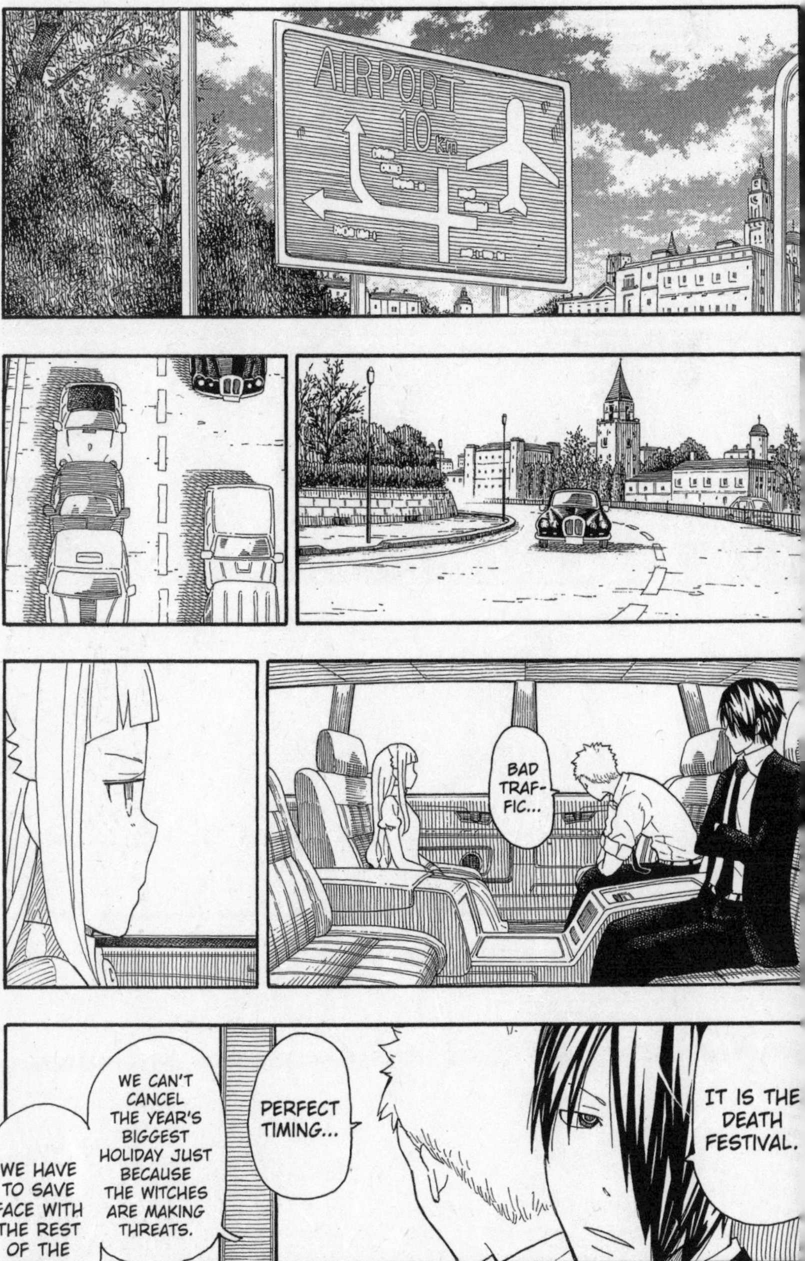
AIRPORT
10 Km
BAD TRAF-FIC...
IT IS THE DEATH FESTIVAL.
PERFECT TIMING...
WE CAN'T CANCEL THE YEAR'S BIGGEST HOLIDAY JUST BECAUSE THE WITCHES ARE MAKING THREATS.
WE HAVE TO SAVE FACE WITH THE REST OF THE WORLD.

THE ROYAL FAMILY'S FACE...THE PRINCESS'S FACE...
STU-PID...
DEATH
HEATRE
!?

KILL ...
KILL ...
KILL ...
KILL ...
KILL ...
KILL ...
THIS IS WHERE THE REAL HARVEST BEGINS...

BASASA (FLAP)
NICE ONE, OX-KUN.
GA
GA (KRSH)
GA
BACK AT YOU, TOM-KUN!
GA
BUT IT'S TIME TO SETTLE THIS ONE NOW.
!
WHA—!?
GABA (LUNGE)

HEY!!
DON'T INTERFERE IN OUR MATCH!!
PU (PRICK)
WHAT'S THIS, A BRAWL?
AH... AHH...
ARE THEY DWMA STU-DENTS?
"NOT"s ?
BE CAREFUL. SOME-THING'S WRONG WITH THEM...

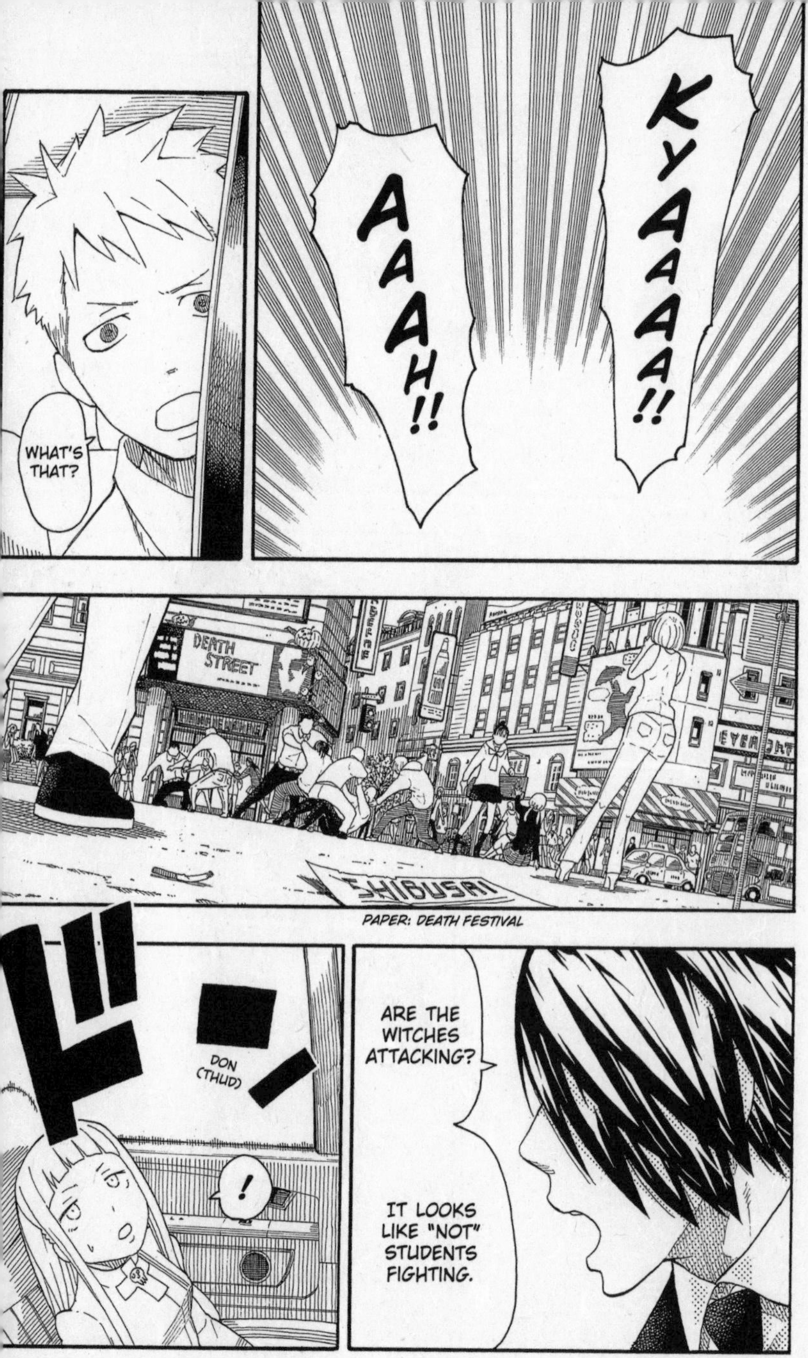
KYAAAAA!!
AAAH!!
WHAT'S THAT?
DEATH STREET
SHIBUSAI
PAPER: DEATH FESTIVAL
ARE THE WITCHES ATTACKING?
IT LOOKS LIKE "NOT" STUDENTS FIGHTING.
DON (THUD)
!

GII (SKREE)
OX!!
YOU GUYS!?
GET IN THE CAR, OX-SENPAI!!
SU (SSK)
DON'T OPEN IT!!
BA (GRAB)
LEAVE THIS TO ME! JUST GET SOMEWHERE SAFE!!

DRIVE!
...A-ALL RIGHT...
KYA
KYA (SQUEAL)
KYA
KYA
VOON (VROOM)
TA (TMP)
GUON (LURCH)
EEEEK!!

ZUGYAGYAGYA (SKREEEEECH)
ALFRED, WHAT IN THE WORLD POSSESSED YOU TO DRIVE LIKE THAT!?
I'VE ALWAYS WANTED TO BE THE HERO OF AN ACTION MOVIE.
BACHI (CRACKLE)
I AM THE BEAST ...
GOGON (BOOOM)
...OF DWMA!!

WHAT'S UP WITH THEM...?
I DON'T CARE WHO THEY ARE. GET IN BLACK☆STAR'S FACE, AND I'LL SEND YOU FLYING.
WHAT'S HAPPEN-ING OUT THERE!?
I WANT A SIT-UATION REPORT!
WE CAN'T GET IN TOUCH WITH ANYONE AT THE DEATH FESTIVAL.
WE'VE GOT POLICE REPORTS POPPING UP ALL OVER!
"NOT" STUDENTS ARE OUT OF CONTROL ALL OVER THE PLACE.
AND THE WITCHES !?
NO REPORTS SO FAR...!!

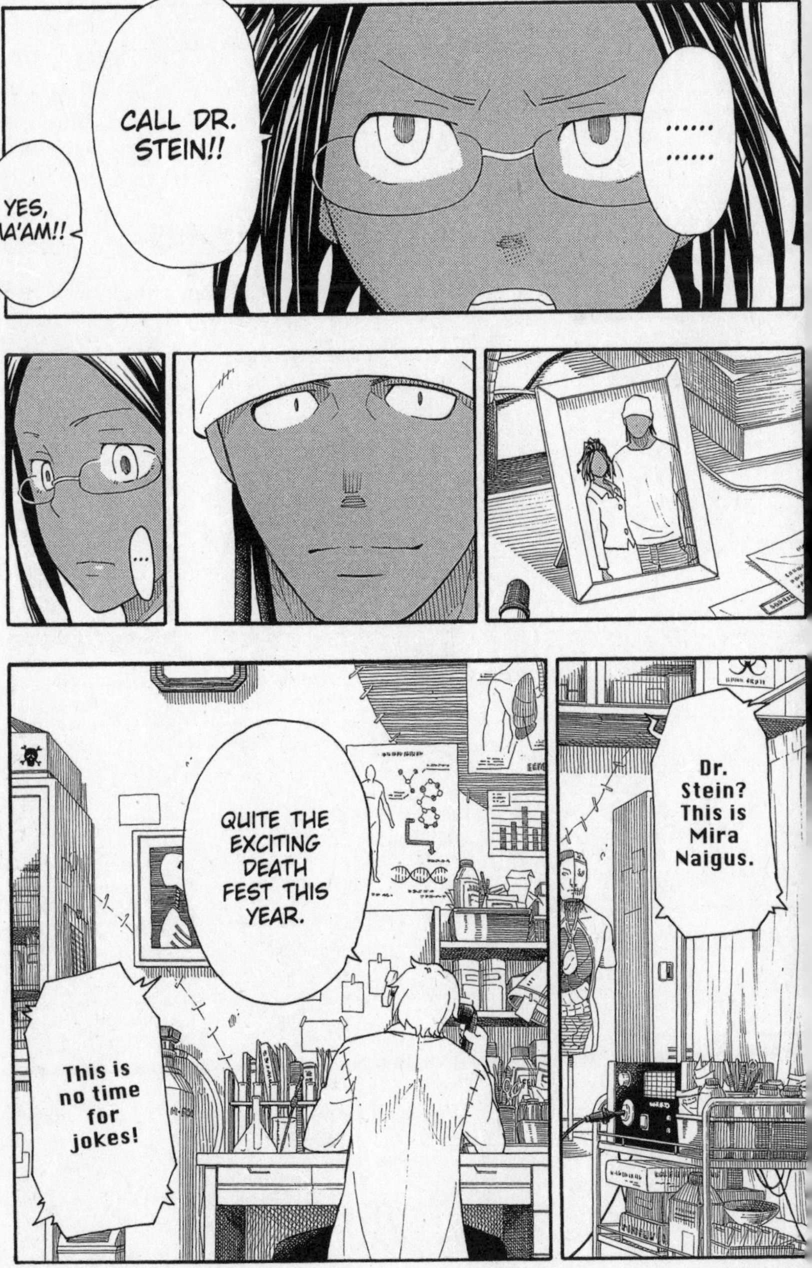
....
CALL DR. STEIN!!
YES, MA'AM!!
...
Dr. Stein? This is Mira Naigus.
QUITE THE EXCITING DEATH FEST THIS YEAR.
This is no time for jokes!

How's the antidote coming?
AFTER COUNTLESS TESTS, I'VE FINALLY FOUND AN EXCELLENT SAMPLE.
ALMOST THERE, I'D SAY.
Make it quick, please!
E·FEATHER
002-13
THEY'RE SO DEMANDING AROUND HERE.

SEALING UP THE GIRLS' DORM!?
I DON'T KNOW THE DETAILS, ONLY THAT THE DEATH FESTIVAL GROUNDS ARE UNDER ATTACK AT MULTIPLE LOCATIONS.
SO THEY MIGHT ATTACK US HERE TOO?
APPARENTLY IT'S THE "NOT"-CLASS STUDENTS WHO ARE DOING THE ATTACKING...
!!
SO IN ORDER TO MINIMIZE THE DAMAGE, NO ONE'S ALLOWED IN OR OUT OF THE DORM...

......
DO YOU THINK IT'S THE WITCHES?
HMM ...
ガシャーン
GASHAN (SLAM)
TSU-GU-MI?
ガチャ
GACHA (KACHAK)
WHAT ARE YOU DOING!?
...
I HAVE TO GO...
MEME-CHAN COULD BE OUT THERE!

DON'T! YOU CAN'T LEAVE THE DORM RIGHT NOW.
BESIDES, YOU'RE ON PER-SONAL CURFEW.
STILL, I HAVE TO GO...MEME-CHAN'S WAITING FOR ME...
WHAT CAN YOU EVEN DO ON YOUR OWN?
I'M NOT ALONE! I'VE GOT ANYA-SAN!
SHE LEFT FOR THE AIRPORT A WHILE AGO.
BUT I... MADE A PROMISE.
I SWORE I WOULD CHOOSE EITHER ANYA-SAN OR MEME-CHAN AS MY PARTNER BY TODAY...
I HAVEN'T TOLD THEM MY ANSWER YET...
HAVE YOU MADE YOUR DECISION?

DOSU (THUD)
NOT YET.
OUCH...
LOOK, JUST CHILL OUT...
BUT... I THINK I CAN TELL.
ANYA-SAN WOULDN'T GO BACK HOME AND LEAVE US BEHIND...
WHEN CLAY-KUN YELLED AT HER, I THINK SHE WAS REALLY ANGRY.
ANGRY THAT THESE DECISIONS HAD BEEN MADE AND KEPT SECRET FROM HER...AND ANGRY THAT SHE HADN'T REALIZED IT...
SHE WAS SO ANGRY AND FRUSTRATED THAT SHE DIDN'T EVEN TURN AROUND WHEN I CALLED TO HER!
BUT...

...SHE JUST DIDN'T WANT ANYONE TO SEE...
...HER TEARS OF FRUSTRA-TION...
BUT THAT'S JUST YOUR ASSUMP-TION. IT DOESN'T MEAN IT'S THE...
I KNOW!
I DON'T KNOW FOR SURE, BUT I KNOW!
SOUL RESO-NANCE...
!
?
KIM...
GOOD GRIEF...

Tanoon-coon, raccoon-coon.
PAAAA (GLOW)
Pom pom, pom kinuta.
PON (PAT)
DON'T GET AHEAD OF YOURSELF, WIMP.
ACK!
HUH?
MY BODY FEELS LIGHT...
YOU HAVEN'T HAD ANY SLEEP, HAVE YOU?
THAT WAS A CHARM TO MAKE YOU FEEL BETTER.
WOW!
THANK YOU. ♪

DON'T ATTEMPT THE IMPOSSIBLE! RUN AWAY IF IT GETS DANGEROUS!!
I WILL...
TA (TAK)
TA
YOU SURE?
I KNOW WHAT IT FEELS LIKE TO WANT TO BREAK THE RULES TO HELP SOMEONE YOU CARE ABOUT.
SAYS THE HARD-ASS.
WHAT ARE YOU SO AFRAID OF?
BISHI (SMAK)
BISHI
TO (TOK)
TO

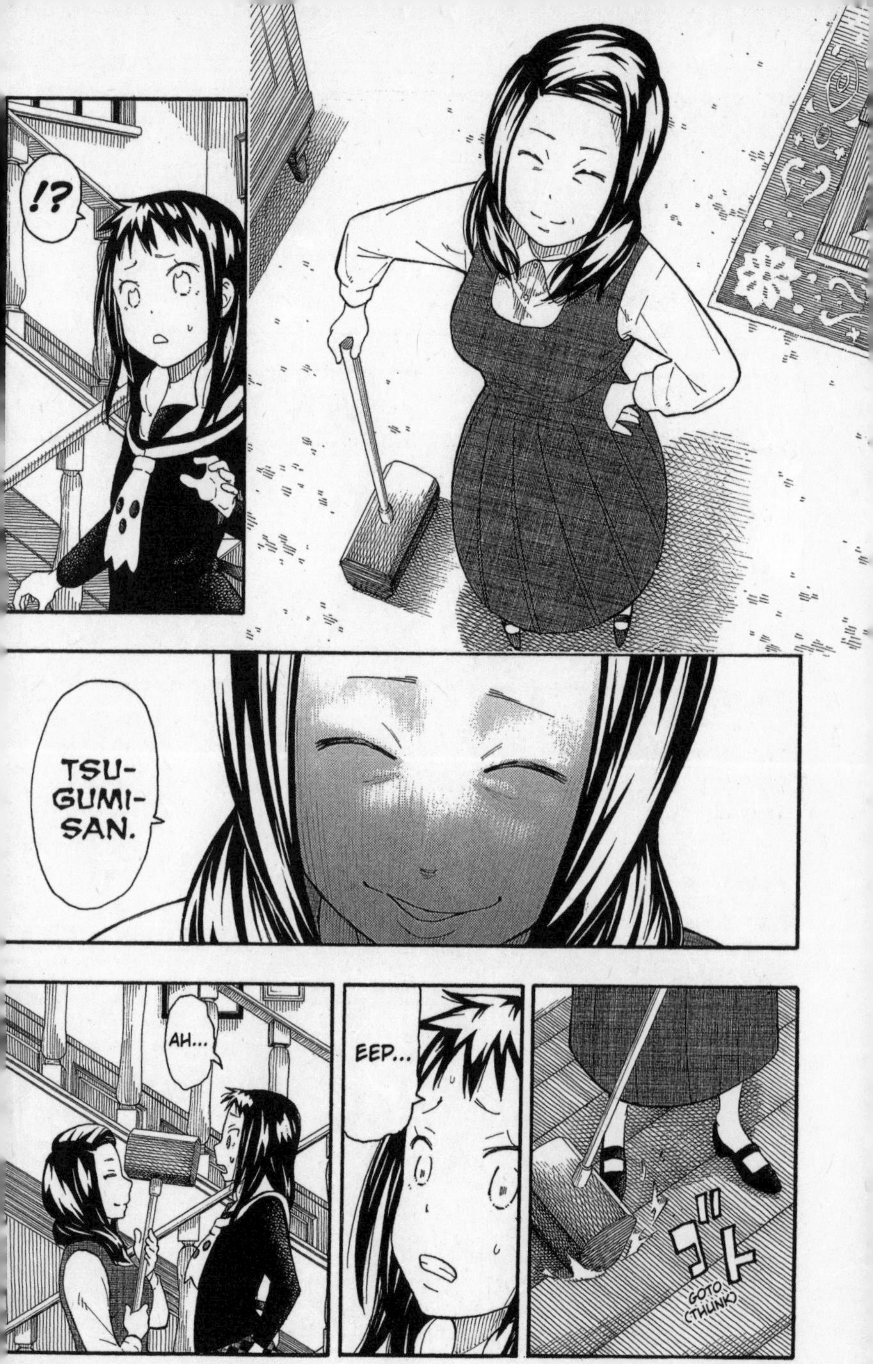
!?
TSU-
GUMI-
SAN.
AH...
EEP...
ゴト
GOTO
(THUNK)

MISS SUPER ...
I'M SORRY, BUT I HAVE TO DO THIS!!
IT'S FINE. JUST GO.
ぱっ
PA (FWP)
HUH?
That spunk, that energy...
...that's the Commoner of Flanders I love so much!
HUFF! HUFF!
You're the Mary I've always sought!!
OH...
WANT THIS?
NO, THANK YOU...

HANG ON! I'M COMING, ANYA-SAN!
MEME-CHAN!!

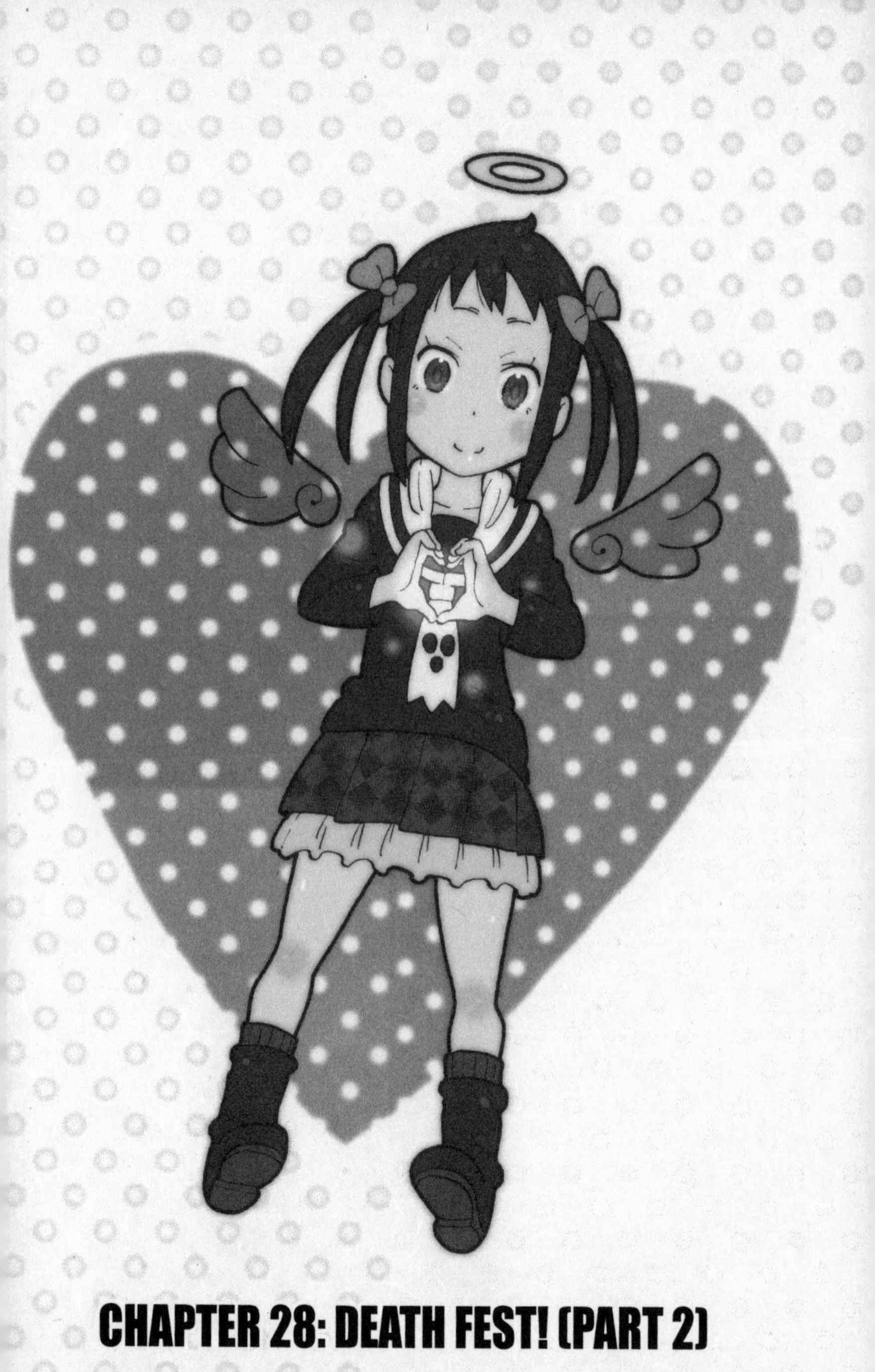

CHAPTER 28: DEATH FEST! (PART 2)

STOP THE CAR.
HUH?
I NEED TO BE WITH TSUGUMI-SAN RIGHT NOW.
NOT THIS AGAIN...
HOW CAN I RUN BACK HOME WHEN SOMEONE SO DEAR TO ME IS SUFFERING WITHOUT MY SUPPORT!?

SOUL EATER NOT!

CHAPTER 28: DEATH FEST! (PART 2)

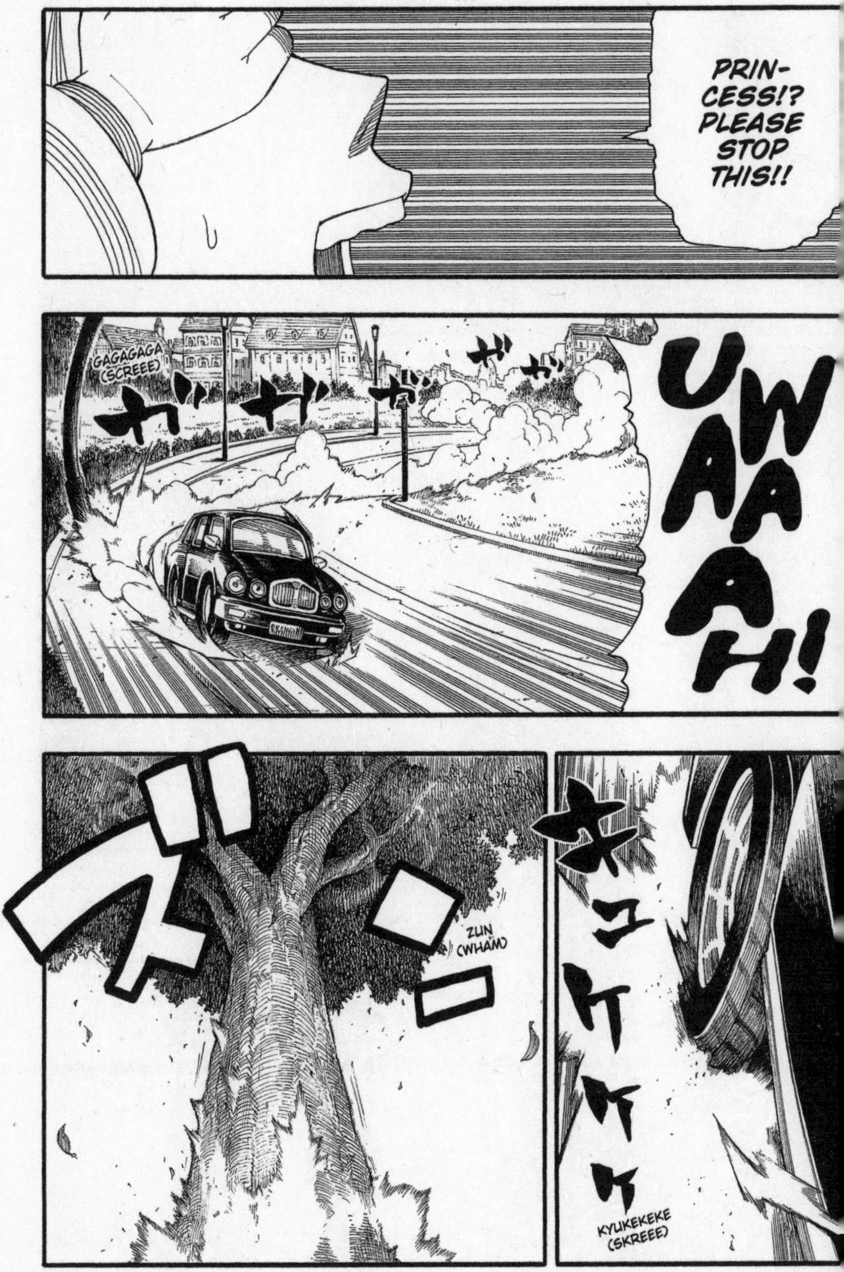
PRIN-
CESS!?
PLEASE
STOP
THIS!!
UWAAAAH!
GAGAGAGA
(SCREEE)
KYUKEKEKE
(SKREEE)
ZUN
(WHAM)

KYAAAA!!
ガガーン
GAGAN (WHAM)
AAAAAH!!
ガシャン
GASHAN (CRASH)
SOUNDS LIKE THE DEATH FEST IS GETTING GOOD.
IT'S MORE EXCITING THAN I FIGURED IT'D BE...
AAAAH!!
!!
LIZ-SAN, PATTY-SAN!
HFF!
HFF!
THANK GOOD-NESS I FOUND YOU...
OH, TSUGUMI.
WHAT'S THE MATTER...?
HFF!
HFF!
LIZ-SAN... PLEASE...
HFF!
HFF!

HFF!
HFF!
ANYA-SAN... IS ON HER WAY TO THE AIRPORT... TO GO BACK TO HER HOME COUNTRY...
AND I HAVE TO GO SEE HER BEFORE SHE...
HFF!
HFF!
HFF!
SOME STUFF WENT DOWN IN TOWN...
AND THE BUSES AREN'T RUNNING ...
HFF!
BUT IF I DON'T GO NOW ...
HFF!
TSK.
SHUT UP AND GET TO THE DAMN POINT!!
DO (BOOM)

HEY! OLD MAN!! GIVE US YOUR SCOOT-ER, CHUMP!!
DON'T WORRY. WE'RE JUST GONNA BORROW IT, SEE?
HUH?
IS THIS... A STICK-UP?
PUON (VRRM)
KAPO (THUNK)

LOOK, JUST BE GENTLE WITH HER...
I KNOW WHAT I'M DOIN'!!
BUON (VROOM)
MOVE IT!
MOVE IT!
MOVE IT!
GOTTA HAUL ASS FOR THE AIR-PORT!!
GAN (BLAM)
OUTTA THE WAY, OR I'LL PUT A BULLET IN YOUR ASS!!
GAN
...

IT'S TOTALED...
WE'LL HAVE TO CALL FOR ANOTHER CAR.
I'M GOING BACK INTO TOWN.
NO!!
IT'S OUR DUTY TO SEE YOU SAFELY TO THE AIRPORT.
WE CAN'T JUST LET YOU TURN BACK.
DO YOU UNDER-STAND?
AKA-NE-SAN...
IS THAT HOW YOU HONESTLY FEEL, OR JUST LIP SERVICE?
......
IT'S MY DUTY.

IF YOUR "DUTY" MEANS ABANDONING YOUR FRIENDS WHO ARE IN DANGER AND HANDING OVER YOUR BODY AND SOUL...
...THEN YOU SHOULD TOSS THAT CRAP INTO THE SEWER WHERE IT BELONGS!!
IT'S HARD FOR ME TOO...!!
AFTER SID-SENSEI WAS KILLED...
...DIDN'T YOU...
BA (WHOOSH)
...FEEL ANY-THING!?
OF COURSE IT WAS HARD FOR US—
WHAT ARE YOU GOING TO DO BACK IN TOWN?
ISN'T IT OBVIOUS? I'LL TEAM UP WITH TSUGUMI-SAN TO HELP MEME-SAN!
HARUDORI'S ALREADY GIVEN UP.

PECHIN (SMACK)
IS THAT THE KIND OF PERSON YOU THINK SHE IS?
I HAD ASSUMED YOU UNDER-STOOD HER BETTER.
......
......
WE WOULDN'T WANT TO PASS EACH OTHER ON THE WAY...
...SO WE OUGHT TO STAY PUT RIGHT HERE IN EITHER CASE.
?

ANYA-SAAAN!!
PUOOOO (VWOOO)
HOW ...?
HER SOUL ...
I COULD SENSE THAT SHE WAS COMING.
ANYA-SAN!!
BA (LEAP)
ANYA-SAN.
TSU-GUMI-SAN.
I...

WE WERE ONLY APART FOR HALF A DAY, BUT IT FELT LIKE MUCH, MUCH LONGER...
I'M SORRY FOR NOT TELLING YOU ABOUT ALL THIS...
I DIDN'T MEAN TO LIE TO YOU...
IT'S OKAY. YOU DON'T HAVE TO SAY A THING.
!!
I can tell just by holding your hand.
FROM HER SOUL ...?
All of your thoughts and feelings are flowing into me.
MORE IMPORTANTLY, WE NEED TO FIND MEME-CHAN!

WHAT WILL YOU DO IF YOU SUC-CEED?
IF YOU DON'T BREAK SHAULA'S MIND CONTROL, YOU'LL JUST WIND UP KILLING EACH OTHER!
MAYBE I'LL FIND HER BUT WON'T BE ABLE TO HELP...
BUT I CAN'T JUST SIT AROUND AND DO NOTHING.
I HAVE TO TRY... I KNOW YOU FELT THE SAME WAY AFTER SID-SENSEI'S DEATH!!
EVEN SO...
...MAYBE I WON'T BE ABLE TO DO ANY-THING...
MAY WE BORROW THAT SCOOTER, LIZ-SAN?
KNOCK YOURSELF OUT. IT'S NOT MINE ANYWAY.
DO YOU KNOW HOW TO DRIVE IT?
UZU
UZU (TWITCH)
I'VE ALWAYS WANTED TO TRY THIS.
TWIST THE HANDLE-BAR, AND IT'LL GO.
HUH?
IT'S REAL EASY. I USED TO HOTWIRE THIS BABY FOR JOY-RIDES.
LET'S GO!
HUH!?

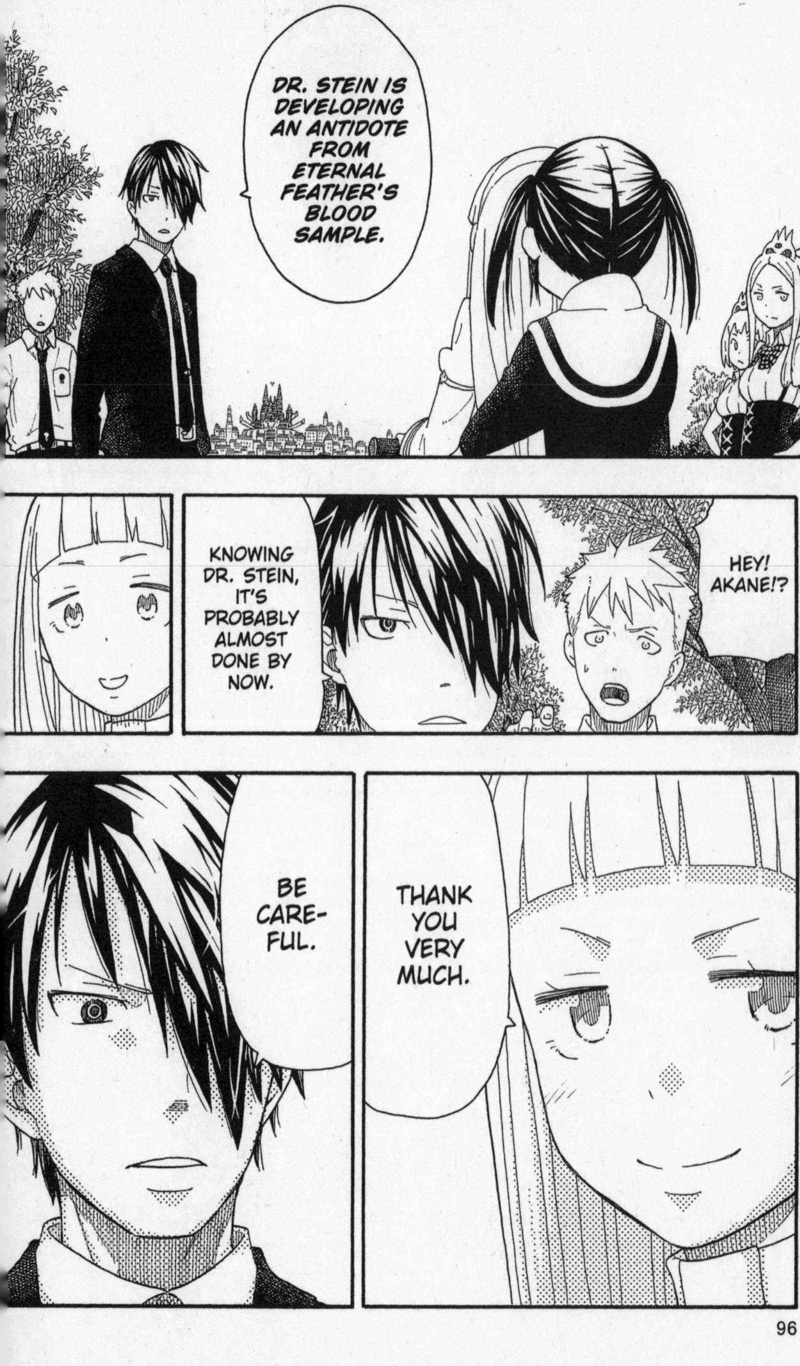
DR. STEIN IS DEVELOPING AN ANTIDOTE FROM ETERNAL FEATHER'S BLOOD SAMPLE.
HEY! AKANE!?
KNOWING DR. STEIN, IT'S PROBABLY ALMOST DONE BY NOW.
THANK YOU VERY MUCH.
BE CARE-FUL.

GUN (TWIST)
WH- WHOA!
BUOOON (VROOOM)
HUHHHH!?
HUHHH!?
YOU DO KNOW THAT WAS TOP SECRET, RIGHT?
AFTER WHAT THEY SAID ABOUT SID-SENSEI...
...COULD YOU HAVE STOPPED THEM, CLAY?
AND WE CAN'T LET THEM WANDER AROUND WITHOUT ANY DIRECTION.

C'MON, LET'S GET BACK TO TOWN TOO.
THIS IS A MATTER OF VEN-GEANCE.
IT'S TIME TO STRIKE DOWN SHAULA THE WITCH.
YOU GOT IT!!

PHEW.
MADE IT IN TIME SOME-HOW.
EEEK!! ANYA-SAN!!
SLOW DOWN! BRAKES! HIT THE BRAKES !!
?
DON (BOOM)
OH?
WEL-COME.

I SEE.
YOU'VE COME FOR THE ANTIDOTE.
YES. SO MAY WE HAVE IT?
HMM.
WELL, THAT'S A TRICKY QUES-TION...
WHAT? WHY AREN'T YOU HELPING?
THERE'S NO TIME TO WASTE!
THERE ARE TWO REASONS I SHOULDN'T GIVE THIS TO YOU...
ONE, THIS SOLUTION BREAKS DOWN THE POISON WITHIN THE BODY, BUT ITS EFFECT ON MENTAL CONTROL IS AS YET UNKNOWN.
IT'S ENTIRELY POSSIBLE THAT IT WON'T WORK AT ALL...
WORST CASE SCENARIO, IT COULD BE FATAL.

FATAL !?
JUST KIDDING.
SHUBIBIN (FWOOSH)
IS THIS REALLY THE TIME FOR JOKES!?
IS THIS REALLY THE TIME FOR FLYING !?
WE'RE IN A TERRIBLE RUSH!
TWO, NAIGUS-SENSEI IS COMING HERE FROM DWMA TONIGHT TO PICK UP THE SAMPLE.
ONCE SHE'S TESTED THE SAMPLE TO MAKE SURE IT WORKS...
...THEN IT CAN BE MASS-PRODUCED, AND IN THREE DAYS—
THREE DAYS...?
WHAT IF SOMETHING HAPPENS TO MEME-CHAN BEFORE THEN!?
KA (TOK)
KA
GII (CREAK)
DR. STEIN!!

I'M HERE FOR THE SA—
!
WHAT ARE YOU DOING HERE?
WE'VE COME TO TAKE THE ANTIDOTE SO WE CAN SAVE MEME-SAN...
AREN'T YOU SUPPOSED TO BE ON YOUR WAY TO THE AIRPORT? YOU NEED TO FOLLOW INSTRUCTIONS—DON'T MAKE THIS MORE COMPLICATED.
WE'LL GO AND TEST THE MEDICINE ON MEME-SAN TO SEE IF IT WORKS...
DON'T BE RIDICULOUS! WHAT DO YOU THINK YOU GIRLS CAN POSSIBLY DO?
TRUST IN US! WE'RE FIGHTING THE SAME ENEMY!
OUR ENEMY IS THE SAME, BUT WHAT WE'RE FIGHTING TO PROTECT IS DIFFER-ENT!

ヒュ
HYU
(SWISH)
ポ
PO
(PLOP)

WAIT, THAT'S SUP-POSED TO BE—
MAKE HER DRINK IT, AND THE NEUTRAL-IZATION OF THE POISON WILL BEGIN RIGHT AWAY.
NOW GET GOING.
PATA (WAVE) PATA
THANK YOU!
WE'LL BRING MEME-SAN BACK—WE SWEAR!
WAIT A MIN—
TA (TEK) TA
WHAT ARE YOU DOING? WHY WOULD YOU GIVE IT TO THEM!?
WE'LL GO RETRIEVE IT.
NOW, NOW, SETTLE DOWN...
GOSO (RSTL) GOSO
GARA (CLINK)
DON (WHUMP)
......

ISN'T IT JUST TOO MUCH FUN TO TEASE THEM?
AND YOU.
KOPU (SLOSH)
......
IT SEEMS THE ENTIRE CITY IS IN A STATE OF CHAOS. WHERE COULD MEME-SAN BE...?
I DOUBT WE'LL BE ABLE TO FIND HER BY RUNNING AROUND AT RANDOM.
BUT WE DON'T HAVE ANY CLUES...
GOSO (RUMMAGE)
ALL I HAVE IS THIS.
THIS?
SU (SWISH)
MEME-CHAN'S BAT WHISTLE.

MES-SEN-GER BAT!
PUSHUUU (FWOOT)
NOW WE JUST FOLLOW THE BATS...
BASA (FLAP)
BASA
LET'S GO!!

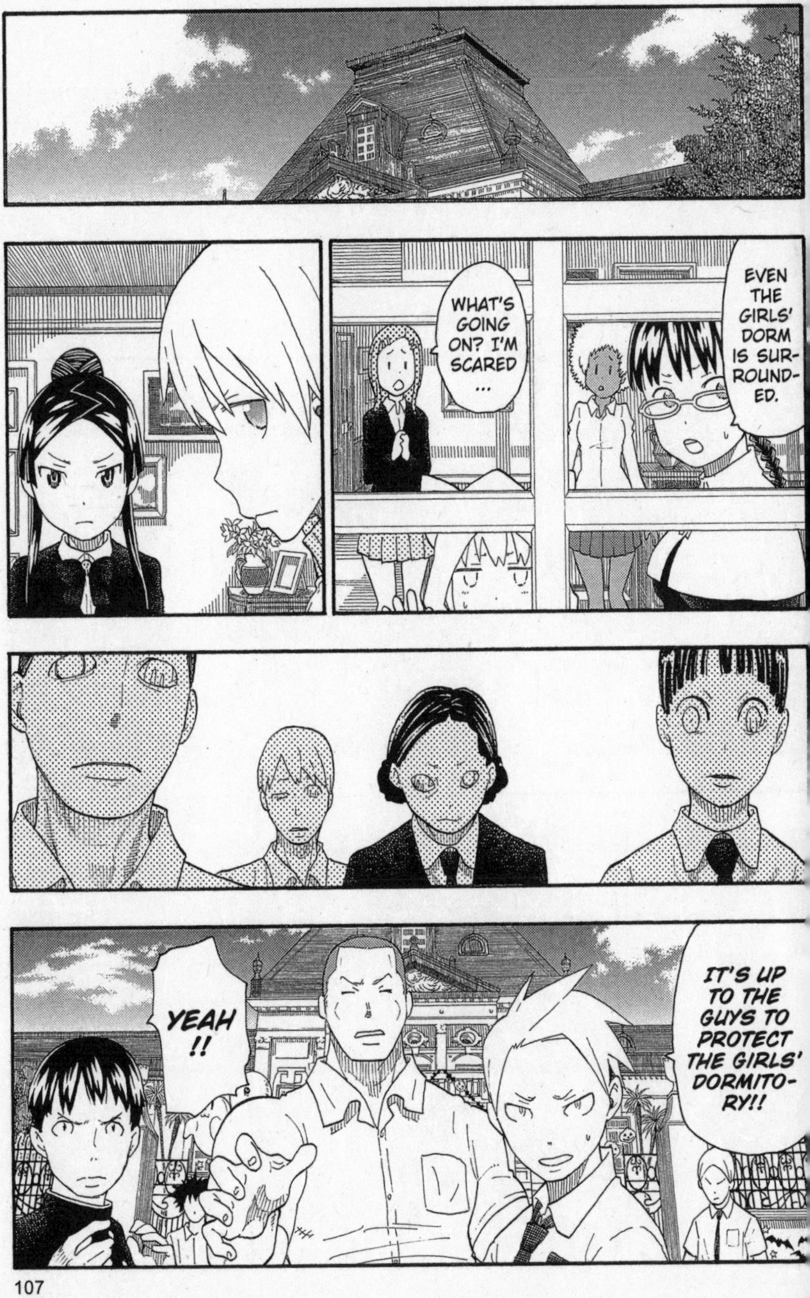
EVEN THE GIRLS' DORM IS SUR-ROUND-ED.
WHAT'S GOING ON? I'M SCARED ...
IT'S UP TO THE GUYS TO PROTECT THE GIRLS' DORMITO-RY!!
YEAH !!

GO ON, MURDER ONE ANOTHER!!
LET THE TOWN BE PAINTED IN YOUR BLOOD! LET ORDER TURN TO MADNESS!!
!
PATA (FLAP)
PATA
BASA (FLAP)
MEME-SAN!!

MEME-CHAN!!
KILL ....!!

SOUL EATER NOT!

KILL.
KILL.
KILL.
KILL.
BOTA (DRIP)
MEME-CHAN, CAN YOU HEAR ME!?
ARE YOU ALL RIGHT, MEME-SAN!?

SOUL EATER NOT!

CHAPTER 29: DEATH FEST! (PART 3)

HEH HEH HEH.
I HADN'T EXPECTED YOU TO FIND US HERE.
SO YOU MUST BE SHAULA.
GIVE BACK MEME-CHAN!!
HOW DE-LIGHT-FUL.
YOU WANT ME TO LET YOU JOIN HER NOW?
I HEAR YOU'RE HAVING TROUBLE SELECTING YOUR PART-NER...
...TSU-GUMI-CHAN?
PERON (LICK)
...HOW DID YOU KNOW THAT?
DON'T TOUCH MEME-SAN!

SHALL I DECIDE FOR YOU?
?
SU (SWISH)
SU
I CAN MAKE THE CHOICE EASIER IF I ELIMINATE ONE OF YOUR OPTIONS.
!!
NO, STOP!!
PFFT!
HA! HA! HA-HA-HA! YOU'RE HILARI-OUS!!
YOU DON'T REALIZE THAT THE MORE FRIENDS YOU HAVE, THE MORE WEAKNESSES YOU HAVE... DIDN'T YOU LEARN THAT FROM ETERNAL FEATHER?

IF YOU JUST GIVE UP YOUR EMO-TIONS...
...YOU CAN BE FREE.
THAT'S HER... SHAULA THE WITCH!!
DAN (WHAM)
TSUGUMI-SAN, GET READY TO USE IT.
OKAY!
SHE'S THE ONE WHO MA-NIPULATED ETERNAL FEATHER-SENPAI...
WE'RE GONNA SAVE YOU NOW, MEME-CHAN.
GU (SQUEEZE)
KILL.

...AND TRIED TO TEAR US APART!
DO IT, MEME! YOU ARE FREE!! KILL YOUR FORMER FRIENDS AND SHED ALL FETTERS!!
DA (DASH)
TSUGUMI-SAN, DODGE!
PAN (SMAK)
NGH!
PAN

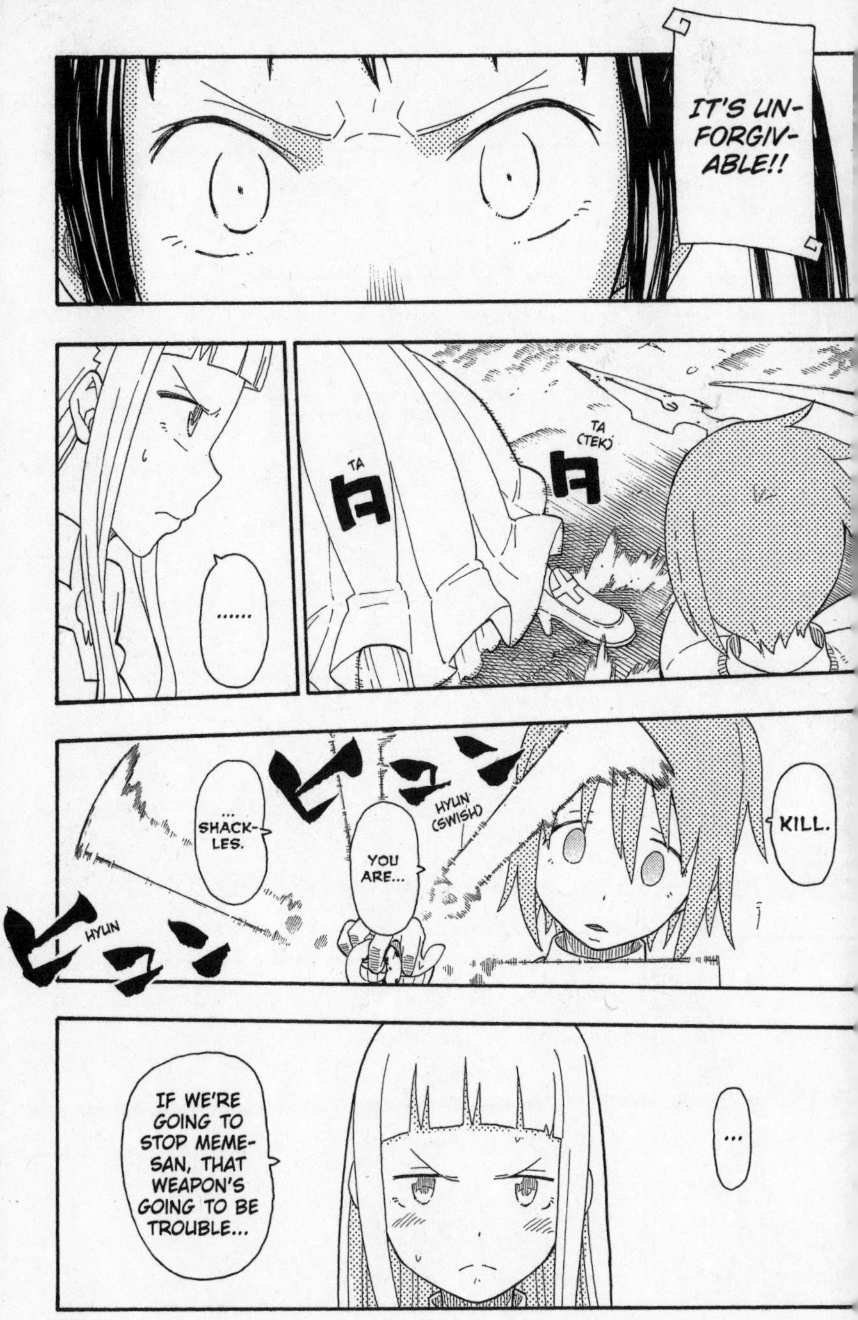
IT'S UN-FORGIV-ABLE!!
TA (TEK)
TA
......
KILL.
HYUN (SWISH)
YOU ARE...
... SHACK-LES.
HYUN
...
IF WE'RE GOING TO STOP MEME-SAN, THAT WEAPON'S GOING TO BE TROUBLE...

BIRI (RRRIP)
BIRIRI
SO I'LL TANGLE UP HER WEAPON IN CLOTH!
IT GOES AGAINST THE ELEGANCE OF ROYAL MARTIAL ARTS, BUT THIS IS A REAL STREET FIGHT!
HYUN (SWISH)
!
HYUN
PASHI (SNATCH)
TSU-GUMI-SAN!!
MMM.

!
KORO (ROLL)
VERY WELL.
I'M A DWMA STUDENT TOO!!
SO YOU TURN YOUR WEAPON ON YOUR FRIEND!
HOW CRUEL AND UNFEEL-ING OF YOU!
THAT'S RIGHT! KILL EACH OTHER!!
LET EVERY HUMAN BEING IN THIS TOWN FALL INTO ANARCHY AND CHAOS!
OOOOOO (WHOOO)

OOOO (WHOO)
RAAAAH!
MEME-SAN, ARE OUR VOICES REACHING YOU!?
THEY'RE INFECTED ...
THEY JUST KEEP COMING!
SOON YOU WILL UNDERSTAND THE COMFORT AND BLISS OF NOT HAVING EMOTIONS!
THEN YOU CAN SURRENDER YOUR WILL TO ME! EMPTYING YOUR EMOTIONS IS AS REFRESHING AS EMPTYING YOUR BOWELS!
THESE PEOPLE WERE NORMAL A SECOND AGO, BUT NOW THEY'RE CRAZY...
WHAT A PAIN IN THE ASS...

MEME-SAN!!
YAAAAH!
BY TOMORROW, YOU'LL BE MY FAITHFUL SOLDIERS.
AAAH!
GAN (WHAM)

MEME-CHAN...
I KNOW I DON'T HAVE A BLADE...
GIGI (KRRSH)
GUI (YANK)
KAN (KSHING)
...AND THAT I DON'T POSSESS ANY STRENGTH AS A WEAPON.
TATA (TEK)
DA (DASH)

BUT NOW, IN THIS VERY MOMENT...
ROYAL...
...SPEAR-MAN-SHIP!!
OOOO (WHOO)
I DON'T NEED A BLADE!!
HAAAAH!!
I DON'T WANT TO HURT MEME-CHAN!!

MEME-CHAN!!
CHU
CHU (SMOOCH)

ゴク
GOKU (GULP)
ドン
DON (THUMP)
ザザ
ZAZA (SLIDE)
BLEH! BITTER ...
DID YOU DO IT, TSUGUMI-SAN?
I THINK SHE SWALLOWED THE ANTIDOTE!!

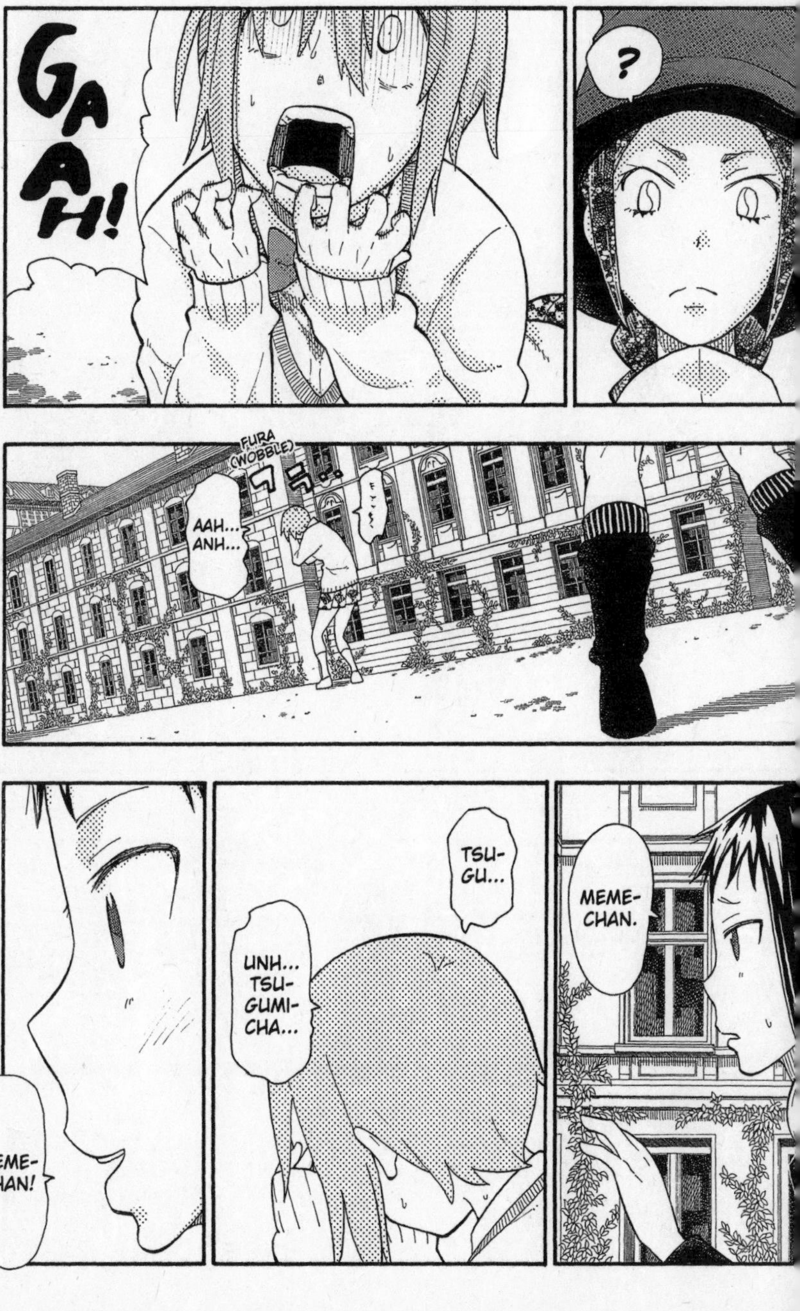
?
GAAH!
FURA (WOBBLE)
AAH... ANH...
MEME-CHAN.
TSU-GU...
UNH... TSU-GUMI-CHA...
MEME-CHAN!

I'LL KILL YOU...
!
!
I DON'T KNOW WHAT YOU GAVE HER, BUT THAT MEAGER ATTEMPT CANNOT OVERCOME MY BRAIN-WASHING!
SUCH SHALLOW BONDS.
"PARTNERS"? "FRIENDS"? THEY'RE ONLY TOOLS TO FILL THE EMPTINESS WITHIN YOUR HEARTS.
"SOULS"? "RESONANCE"? DON'T MAKE ME LAUGH! THIS TOWN OVERFLOWS WITH HIDEOUS HYPOCRISY.

MEME-CHAN!! DON'T FORGET US!!
YOU WOULD NEVER DO THIS SORT OF THING TO US!!
カチャ
KACHA (CLINK)
ヒュ
HYU (SWISH)
SHUT UP!!
GET BACK, TSUGUMI-SAN.
NO, IT'S FINE.
DO YOU REMEMBER, MEME-CHAN?
REMEMBER THE TIMES WE COOKED TOGETHER AND WORKED AT THE CAFÉ?

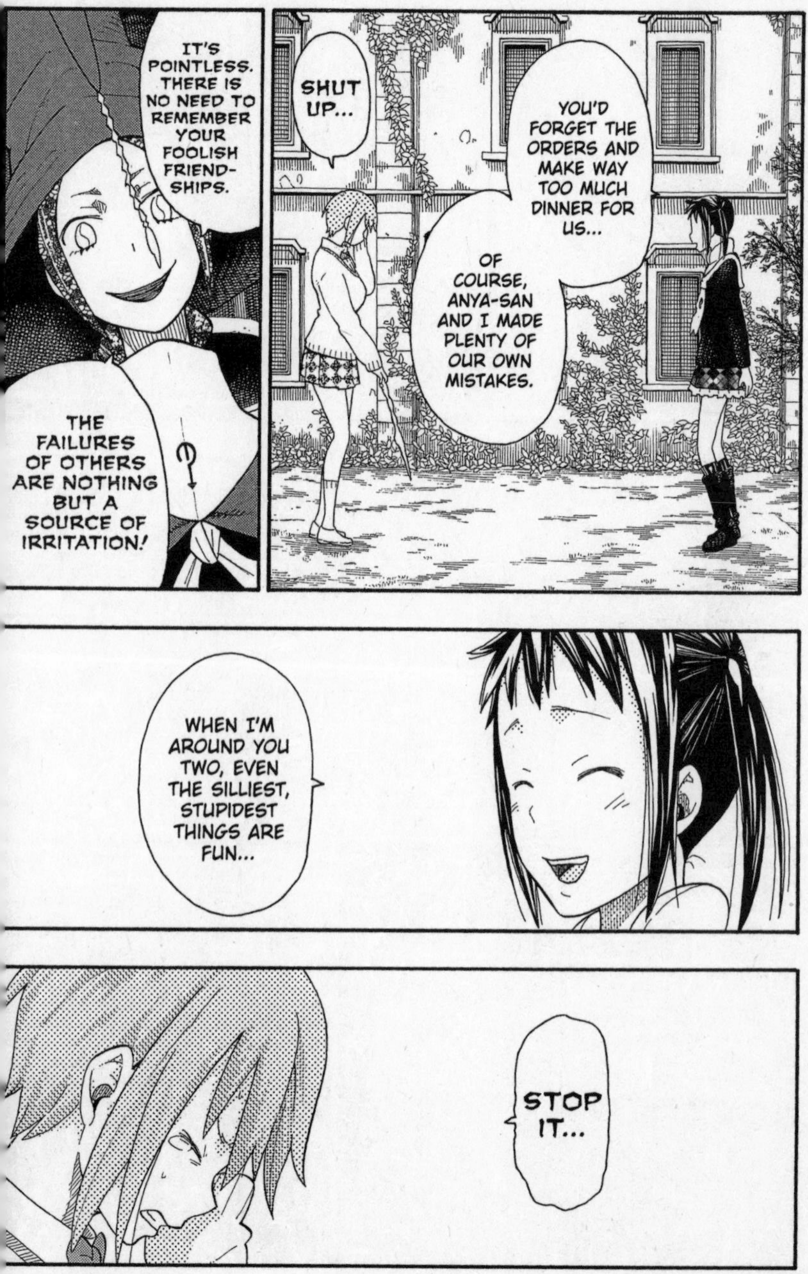
YOU'D FORGET THE ORDERS AND MAKE WAY TOO MUCH DINNER FOR US...
OF COURSE, ANYA-SAN AND I MADE PLENTY OF OUR OWN MISTAKES.
SHUT UP...
IT'S POINTLESS. THERE IS NO NEED TO REMEMBER YOUR FOOLISH FRIEND-SHIPS.
THE FAILURES OF OTHERS ARE NOTHING BUT A SOURCE OF IRRITATION!
WHEN I'M AROUND YOU TWO, EVEN THE SILLIEST, STUPIDEST THINGS ARE FUN...
STOP IT...

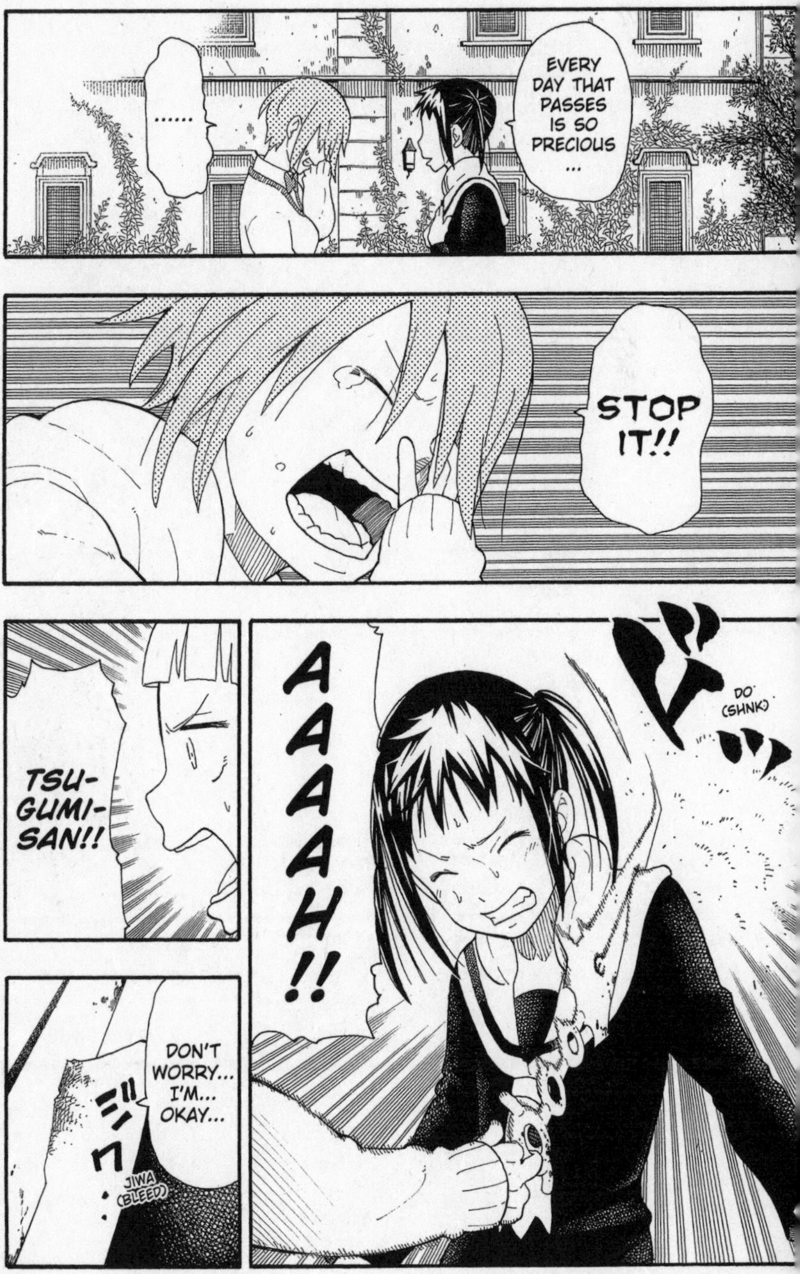
EVERY DAY THAT PASSES IS SO PRECIOUS ...
......
STOP IT!!
DO (SHNK)
AAAAAH!!
TSU-GUMI-SAN!!
DON'T WORRY... I'M... OKAY...
JIWA (BLEED)

THAT'S RIGHT, MEME! KILL HER!!
IT WAS NEVER FUN! SHOW THAT GIRL YOU'RE NOT JUST A TOOL TO GIVE HER ENTERTAIN-MENT!!
SHUT UP!!
DON'T STEAL MEME-CHAN'S MEMORIES.
THOSE IRREPLACEABLE MEMORIES OF THE THREE OF US TOGETHER...
IT'S NOT JUST FOR ME...THOSE MEMORIES BELONG TO ALL THREE OF US...WE ALL HAVE TO REMEMBER THEM...

I NEED TO APOLOGIZE TO YOU, MEME-CHAN.
I SHOULDN'T HAVE SAID THOSE THINGS!
JUST COME BACK!!
BACK TO THE NICE, FLUFFY, DITZY MEME-CHAN!
I DON'T CARE HOW MANY TIMES YOU FORGET THINGS.
I'LL APOLOGIZE OVER AND OVER AND OVER AGAIN...
...FOR HURTING YOUR FEELINGS.
I'M SORRY...
BORO (DRIP)

ピ!!!
PISHI
(KRACK)

?
TON (TMP)
MEME-CHAN?
HARU-DORI-SAN...
MEME-SAN!?
TA (TEK)
PIKU (TWITCH)

I heard your voices...
I...
I didn't forget...
MY MIND CONTROL...
...WAS BROKEN?
WHAT... HAVE I DONE?

MEME TATANE! HAVE YOU LOST YOUR SENSES? THINK, GIRL!
WHO IS YOUR MASTER? YOUR MOTHER? YOUR FUNES? YOUR LOVER? YOUR FRIEND?
ISN'T IT... ME?
YOU CAN'T PRETEND TO HAVE FORGOTTEN. YOU KILLED SID.
THE WORLD WILL CURSE YOU, PUSH YOU AWAY... BUT I FORGIVE YOU. I FORGIVE YOU FOR EVERY-THING.
I AM EVERY-THING TO YOU.
DO NOT LET THESE GIRLS LEAD YOU ASTRAY BY PRETENDING TO BE YOUR FRIENDS.

UO
(VWOOSH)
GOOON
(GONGGG)
SHUT UP...

I MIGHT NOT BE THE SAME ME THAT YOU GUYS KNOW...
GOOOOON
...BUT I WON'T FORGET THE REAL ME AGAIN!!
THE HARD TIMES, THE FUN TIMES...
THE MEMORIES OF MY TWO FAVORITE PEOPLE...
I WON'T FORGET THE IMPORTANT THINGS EVER AGAIN!!

SOUL EATER NOT!

AAAH!
WHOA!!
ポタ
POTA (DRIP)
ポタ
POTA
THEY'RE BEING INFECTED BY THE ONES WITH THAT CLAW FINGER RING...
AAAH!
!
ROYAL KARATE!!
DO (WHUMP)

GOOON (GONGGG)
ゴォォン
ゴォォォン
GOOOON
......
WHY IS THE BELL RINGING NOW?
THIS FEELING IN THE AIR...
DA (DASH)
LET'S GO!!

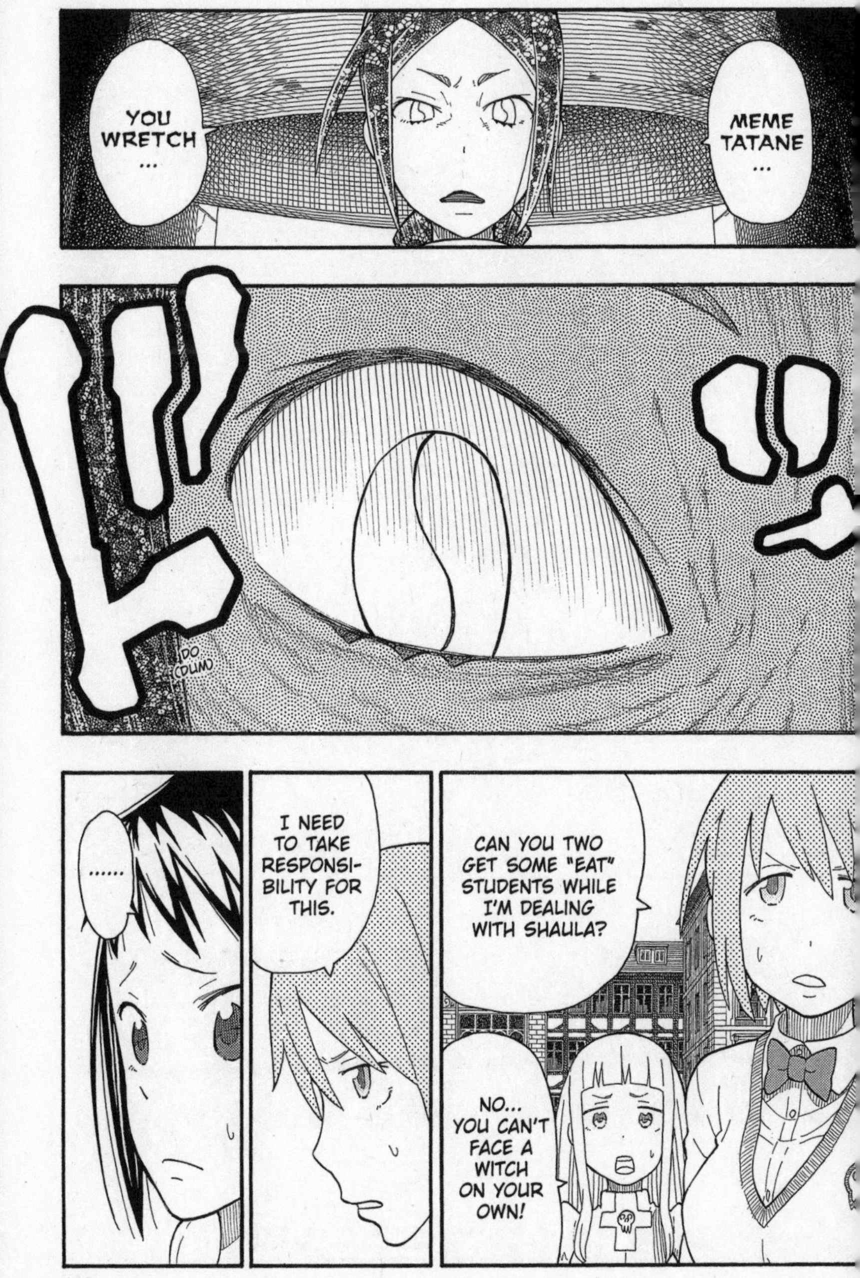
MEME TATANE ...
YOU WRETCH ...
!!
DO (DUM)
CAN YOU TWO GET SOME "EAT" STUDENTS WHILE I'M DEALING WITH SHAULA?
NO... YOU CAN'T FACE A WITCH ON YOUR OWN!
I NEED TO TAKE RESPONSIBILITY FOR THIS.
......

SOUL EATER NOT!

CHAPTER 30: DEATH FEST! (PART 4)

I KNOW WHO I'M TAKING AS MY PARTNER ...
WHY ARE YOU BRINGING THIS UP NOW...?
......
ANYA-SAN!

MEME-CHAN.
I'M MAKING YOU BOTH MY PARTNERS.
WHAT ARE YOU TALKING ABOUT? TWO PEOPLE CAN'T USE ONE WEAPON.
WHEN WE ALL GOT SEPARATED, I REALIZED SOMETHING— I CAN'T DO ANYTHING ON MY OWN.
WHETHER WE FIGHT OR RUN, I CAN'T STAND THE THOUGHT OF LEAVING ONE OF US BEHIND.

WE'RE AT OUR STRONGEST...
...WHEN WE'RE TOGETHER!
ONCE WE WERE REUNITED LIKE THIS, I HAD AN EPIPHANY.
WE CAN SHARE "SOUL RESONANCE" TOGETHER!!
I HAVE ENOUGH SOLDIERS NOW.
BASA (FLAP)
BASA
ALL THREE OF YOU WILL DIE HERE.

DAN (THUMP)
DO YOU TWO ...
...NOT WANT TO BE A TEAM OF THREE?
IT'S NOT THAT I DON'T...
BESIDES, IT'S NO DIFFERENT FROM WHAT WE'VE BEEN DOING ALL ALONG!
YES, I HAVEN'T FOR-GOTTEN THAT PART...
WE'VE ALWAYS BEEN TOGETHER ...
LET'S DO IT, ANYA-SAN.
EVEN YOU, MEME-SAN?

SEEMS WE HAVE NO TIME TO THINK IT OVER...
SHIRIRIRI (SHREEE)
PASHI (SNATCH)
I CAN FEEL YOUR SOULS!
TWO PEOPLE USING ONE WEAPON? I GUESS THERE'S A FIRST TIME FOR EVERY-THING.

YOU NEED TWO PEOPLE TO HOLD A STICK WITHOUT A BLADE...?
DON'T MAKE ME LAUGH!!
BUO (WHOOSH)
GA (WHACK)
LEAVE THE HEAVY LIFTING TO ME, ANYA-SAN.
GIGI (GRRGH)
YOU FOCUS ON THE COUNTER-ATTACK!!

GOSU
(WHUMP)
SUZAZA
(SKZSH)

PAN
(POW)
DON
(THUD)
GO
(WHAM)

ZAZA
(ZSHH)
DA
(DASH)
THIS IS HOW IT WAS MEANT TO BE! I CAN FEEL OUR SOULS BECOMING ONE!!
HAAAH!!

GA (WHAK)
GA
GA
GA
GA
LITTLE "NOT" BRATS... WHO DO YOU THINK I AM!?
I AM A WITCH.
KOOOOO (WHOOSH)
BUT YOU HAVE MY COMPLIMENTS—YOU FORCED ME TO USE MAGIC, THOUGH YOU WILL SOON REGRET IT!

SCOR-
PION
SCIS-
SORS!!
BA
(WHOOSH)
MEME-
CHAN,
ANYA-
SAN! ARE
YOU ALL
RIGHT!?
CAN YOU SENSE IT? MY POWER IS SO FAR BEYOND YOURS, I COULD OUT-MATCH ANY NUMBER OF YOU.
YOU WILL NOW EXPERIENCE FIRSTHAND WHY THE WITCHES ARE FEARED BY ALL! I WILL NOT HOLD BACK...

...ONLY DE-STROY.
ZOKU (SHIVER)
YOU WOULD HAVE BEEN HAPPIER AS MY FAITHFUL SOLDIERS.
NOW DIE.

BA (WHOOSH)
AKANE-KUN, CLAY-KUN!!
I'M GLAD ALL THREE OF YOU ARE OKAY! LEAVE THIS TO ME AND GET TO SAFETY!

WHAT ARE YOU SAYING? I CANNOT RUN AWAY AND LEAVE BEHIND A FELLOW "NOT" STUDENT.
LET US FIGHT ALONGSIDE YOU.
UH, LISTEN ...
WE TOLD YOU, WE'RE NOT REALLY "NOT" STUDENTS...
THIS IS YOUR PUNISHMENT FOR TRICKING US.
HEY, YOU NEVER SAID YOU WERE A PRINCESS EITHER...
IF WE'RE PLAYING THE BLAME GAME, I PRETTY MUCH LIED TO EVERYONE...
LET'S NOT DO THIS.

IF IT WASN'T FOR SHAULA...
...WE COULD HAVE LAUGHED ALL OF THESE THINGS OFF.
OON (WHMM)
SHE'S RUINED DEATH CITY... THERE'S NOWHERE TO RUN ANYMORE.
OON
AT FIRST, I DIDN'T WANT TO COME TO DWMA.
I WAS NERVOUS AND FRIGHTENED... I HATED THAT I'D BECOME A WEAPON.

BUT ONCE I GOT TO KNOW THE PEOPLE HERE, I REALIZED I WAS HAVING THE TIME OF MY LIFE...
...AND EVERYONE ELSE HELPED A COWARD LIKE ME FIND COURAGE...

SO WHILE EVERYONE ELSE FIGHTS FOR OUR HOME...
...EVEN AS A "NOT," I WANT TO DO MY JOT OF HELP FOR DWMA'S SAKE!
......
WE'RE RESONATING WITH TSUGUMI-SAN, SO WE CAN TELL!
ぎゅっ
GYU (SQUEEZE)
WE FEEL THE SAME WAY!
WE'LL TRY TO EXPOSE SHAULA'S WEAKNESS. WHEN THAT HAPPENS, YOU FINISH HER OFF.
BUT DON'T TRY TO GET IN TOO CLOSE. MAKE USE OF THE HALBERD'S REACH.
FINISH HER OFF? HOW CAN I...?

WHAT DO YOU MEAN?
YOU'VE GOT THAT GORGEOUS EDGE ON YOU, HARUDORI.

I HAVE...
...A BLADE ...
EVEN THE BEST BLADE...
BASA (FLAP)
...IS USELESS WITHOUT THE SKILL AND DETER-MINATION TO STRIKE DOWN THE ENEMY.
MEME-SAN!
ANYA-SAN!

LET'S GO!!
RIGHT!!

SOUL EATER NOT!

ドス
DOSU
(SHOONK)

SOUL EATER NOT!

NAL CHAPTER: IT'S A SAVAGE BUT SUPER-FUN LIFE ♪

DON'T YOU PUSH YOURSELF TOO HARD!!
...
TA (LEAP)
BYA (ZWOOM)

BA
(WHOOSH)
DOGO
(KWAM)

DO
(DOOM)
PA
(SNATCH)
ZUPA
(SLASH)

ZUN (ZMM)
GYURU (SWIVEL)

GA (DSHH)
GA
GA
GA
GA
YOU DIDN'T THINK YOU COULD MURDER SID-SENSEI AND THROW THE WHOLE CITY INTO A PANIC AND GET AWAY WITH IT, DID YOU?
I DON'T NEED TO "GET AWAY"! FROM NOW ON, DEATH CITY WILL BE MY PALACE!
BA (WHOOSH)

THIS IS FOR SID-SENSEI!!
HAAAH !!
BACHI
BACHI (ZZAP)
DO (BOOOM)

ZUZAZA
(SKSHH)
ARE YOU SURE YOU WANT TO DO THIS?
IF YOU ATTACK ME, I CAN FORCE THE HUMANS UNDER MY CONTROL TO COMMIT SUICIDE, ONE AFTER ANOTHER.
JUST LIKE ETERNAL FEATHER.
!
OH NO...
A WORTHLESS THREAT! IF WE DON'T STOP YOU, THESE PEOPLE'S LIVES WILL BE HELL ANYWAY!
DA
(DASH)

GAN (WHAM)
NO MATTER HOW MANY OF US YOU STRIKE DOWN, YOU WILL STILL DIE HERE.
...!
DON'T MESS WITH DWMA.

BA
(LUNGE)
TCH!
SHU
SHU
(SWISH)
SHU
THE PRESSURE OF MY BLADE IS PUSHING SHAULA BACK!
AS LONG AS YOU HAVE AN EDGE, YOUR POWER CAN REPEL THE DARKNESS!

DOGO (THWUD)
MEME ...
...TA-TANE ...
MEKI
MEKI (BLAZE)
I'M DISAPPOINTED IN YOU!
HANG AROUND WITH THESE TWO, AND THEY WILL ALWAYS DRAG YOU DOWN TO THEIR LEVEL!
GU (CLENCH)
OUR FRIENDSHIP ISN'T ABOUT WHO DRAGS DOWN WHOM!

TATANE, YOU'RE TOO CLOSE!!
GA
THEY WILL KEEP YOU FROM BECOMING BETTER THAN YOU ARE NOW!
GA (WHAM)
I WAS TAUGHT MARTIAL ARTS FOR THE PURPOSE OF "BEING BETTER"...
GA
BUT YOU MANIPULATED ME WITH YOUR OWN IDEAS OF WHO'S "BETTER" OR "WORSE"... ALL I HOPE FOR IS THAT MY FISTS WILL HELP THOSE I LOVE BE HAPPY...
GA
SUCH NAIVE NON-SENSE!!
I'M JUST A GIRL TOO, YOU KNOW!!
DO (THWAM)

DOSU (THUD)
KA (KTAK)
TA (TMP)
KUN (FWIP)
KUN
IT SEEMS THAT I'M AT A DIS-ADVANTAGE FIGHTING SOLO. YOU AND MY SOLDIERS CAN KILL EACH OTHER INSTEAD!!

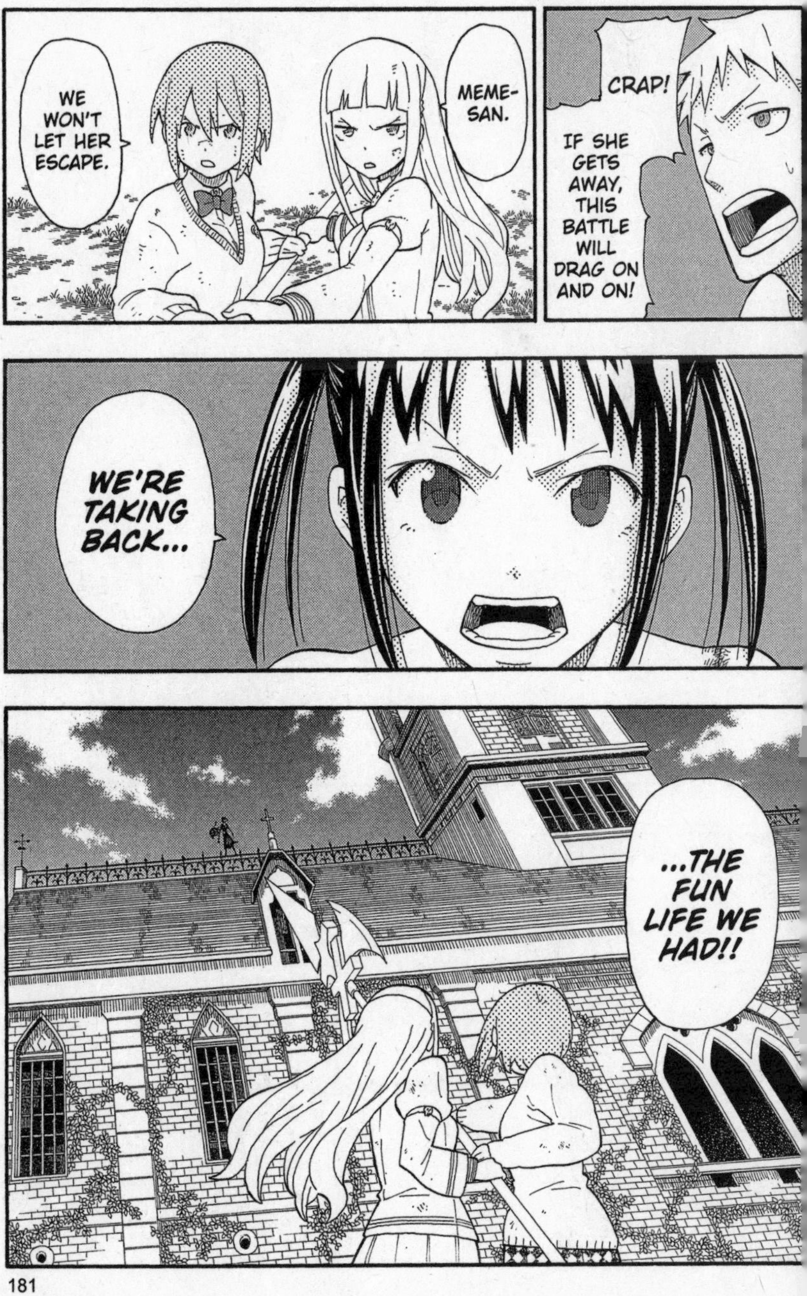
CRAP!
IF SHE GETS AWAY, THIS BATTLE WILL DRAG ON AND ON!
MEME-SAN.
WE WON'T LET HER ESCAPE.
WE'RE TAKING BACK...
...THE FUN LIFE WE HAD!!

KOOOOOOOO
(WHOOOO)
コオオオオオオオ
THE BONDS OF THREE!!!
BECOME A SINGLE SOUL!!!
SHUBAA
(SHWOOSH)
IS THAT SOUL RESONANCE!!?

DO
(BWOOM)

WOW !!
GO FOR IT!!
GOOOO (WHOOM)
WHAT CAN A LITTLE GROUP OF "NOT" GIRLS DO TO ME!?
I'M A WITCH!! I'LL TAKE EVERY-THING YOU HAVE AND GIVE IT BACK DOUBLE!!
BIGU (FLINCH)
!!

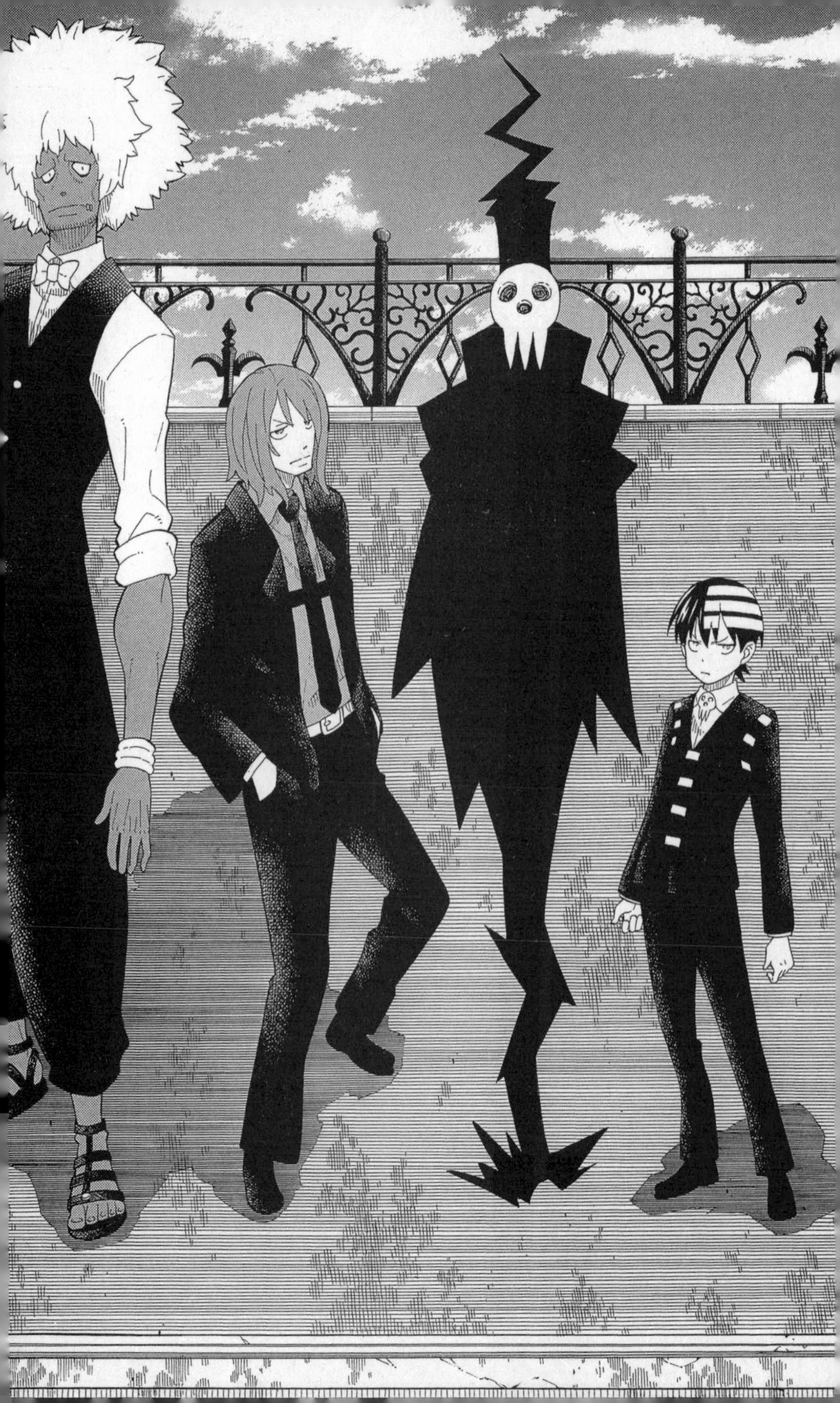

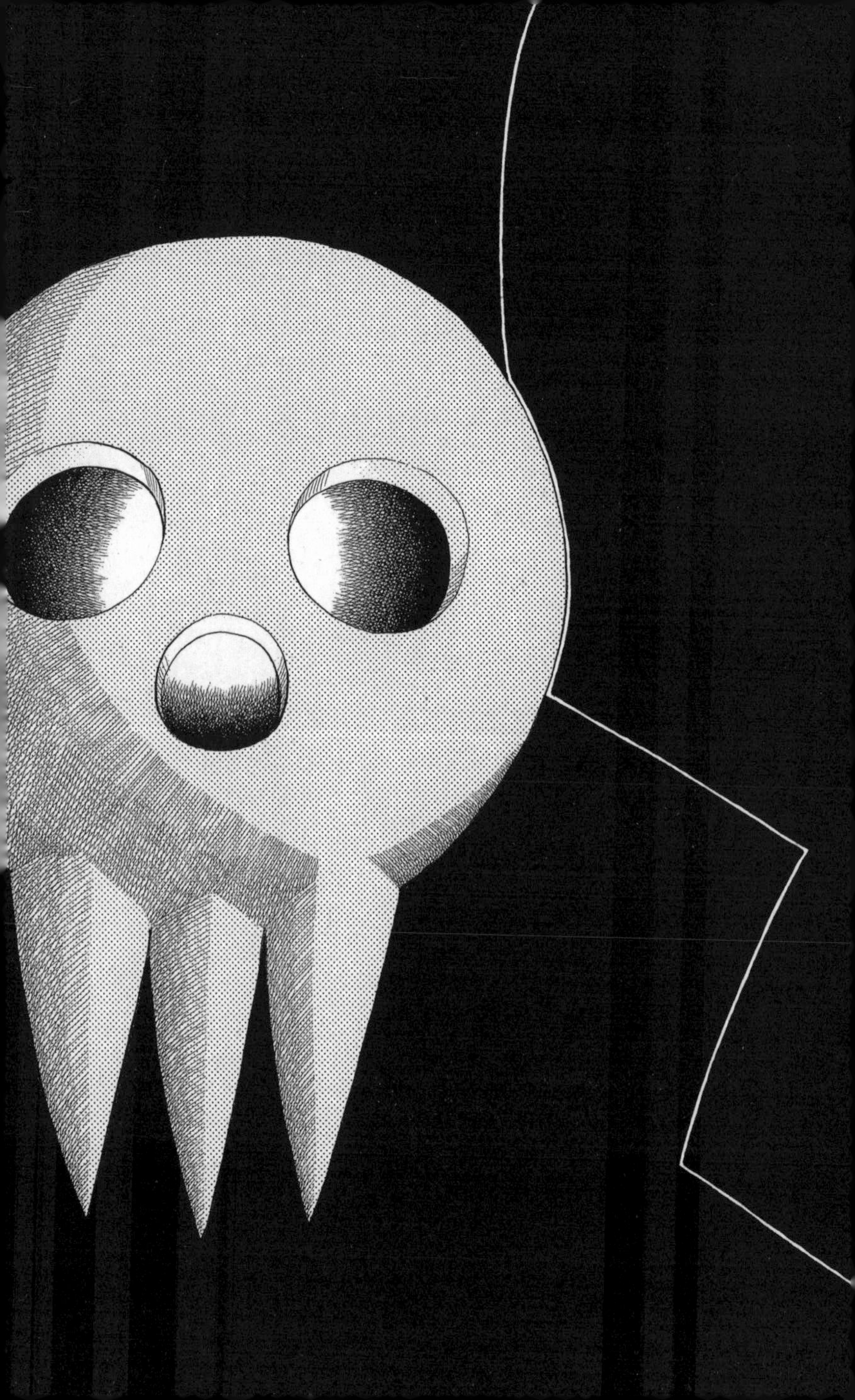

LISTEN, YOU... DO YOU KNOW WHO YOU'VE PICKED A FIGHT WITH?

SHINI...
GAMI...

ズザザザ
ZUZAZAZAZA (ZSHHH)
ペペン
PEPEN (FLUP)
...
......
WE... DID IT?

KOOOO
(WHOOSH)
I'VE GOT SHAULA THE WITCH'S SOUL NOW.
TA
(TEK)
!
THAT WAS AMAZING, YOU THREE!
I MEAN, REALLY BRILLIANT WORK.
IT'S UNPRECEDENTED FOR "NOT" STUDENTS TO DEFEAT A WITCH.
ON TOP OF THAT, I'VE NEVER HEARD OF TWO MEISTERS FOR ONE WEAPON.

I DON'T THINK WE COULD HAVE WON ON OUR OWN...
IT WAS ONLY BECAUSE YOU CREATED AN OPENING FOR US.
WELL, IT SEEMS TO ME...
...YOU'VE DECIDED THE PARTNER QUESTION.
!
きょるきょる
KYORU
KYORU (GLANCE)

Yes!!

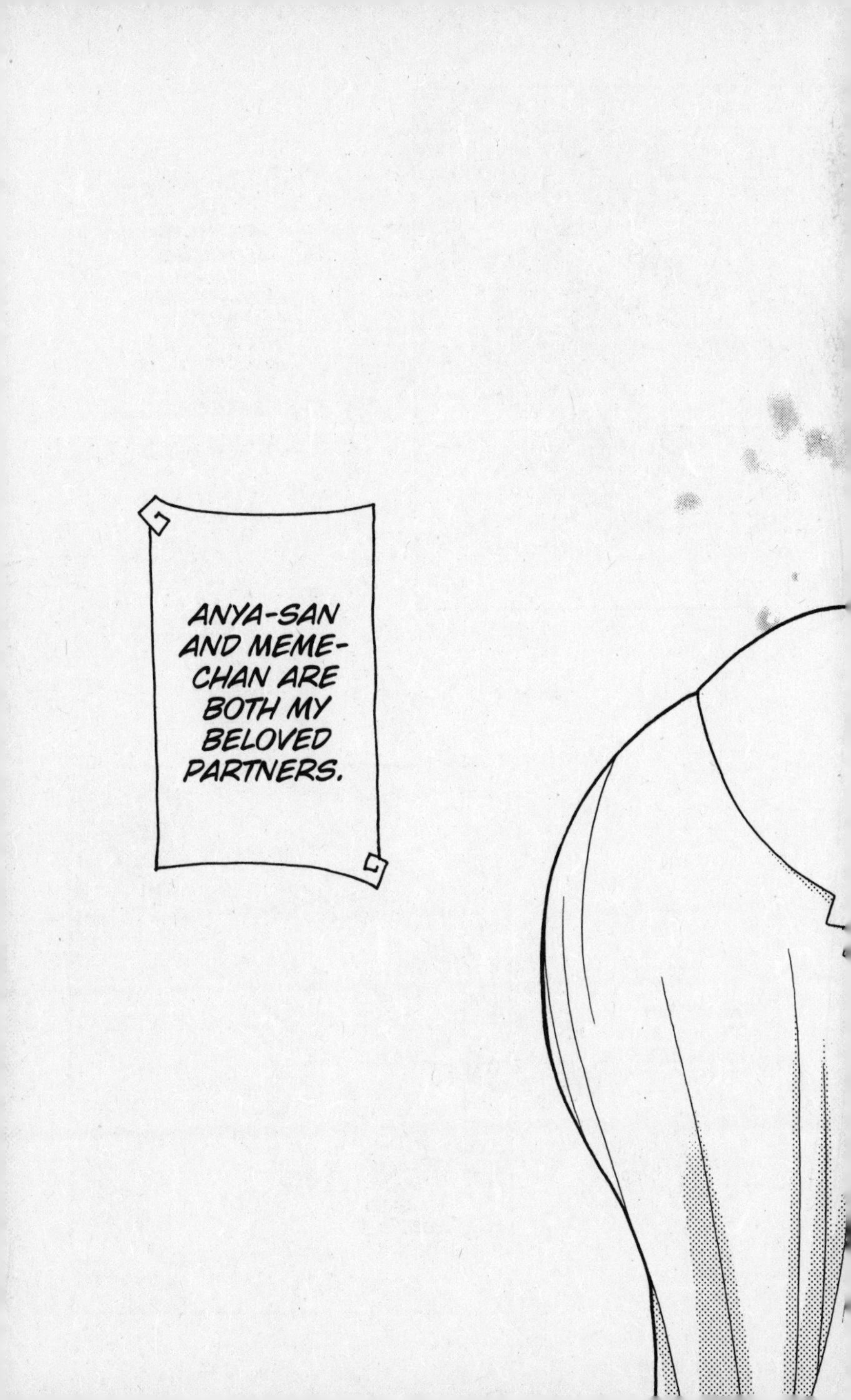
ANYA-SAN AND MEME-CHAN ARE BOTH MY BELOVED PARTNERS.

THE STUDENTS WHO WERE BEING MANIPULATED SEEMED TO REGAIN THEIR SENSES WHEN SHAULA WAS DEFEATED.
THEY COL-LAPSED ...
ARE THEY SLEEP-ING?
THE WITCH'S SIGNAL HAS VANISHED...
WELL, AT LEAST I DON'T HAVE TO DISSECT ANY STUDENTS.
NO DOUBT DR. STEIN WILL HANDLE THE REST!

WE HAD TO SIT THROUGH A LOT OF ANNOYING QUESTIONS AND OTHER FORMALITIES AFTER THAT.

THEY ASKED US STUFF ABOUT SHAULA, BUT BEING "NOT" STUDENTS, WE WEREN'T THAT MUCH HELP IN THE END.

EVEN AFTER THAT TERRIFYING ORDEAL, REGULAR LIFE PICKED UP AGAIN RIGHT AWAY, AND WINTER ARRIVED IN DEATH CITY...
IT'S SO LONELY BEING ALONE IN A THREE-PERSON ROOM...
DEATH CITY, DWMA, AND THE OLDER STUDENTS IN THE GIRLS' DORM ARE ALL BACK TO NORMAL LIKE NOTHING'S WRONG...
THAT'S DWMA FOR YOU, I GUESS.

SADLY, JUST AFTER WE'D DECIDED TO BE TOGETHER, ANYA-SAN HAD TO GO BACK TO HER PARENTS' CASTLE TO REPORT ON WHAT SHE'D BEEN THROUGH.
MEME-CHAN WAS IN THE HOSPITAL FOR A WHILE TO UNDERGO TESTS TO ENSURE THE SPELL HAD WORN OFF. AND SHE HAD TO EXPLAIN WHAT HAPPENED WITH SID-SENSEI... SHE NEEDS A LITTLE TIME.
IT'S LONELY WITHOUT A PARTNER, BUT I CAN USE THIS TIME TO WORK HARD AND TRY TO CATCH UP TO THEIR LEVEL.
I CAN'T ALWAYS BE A FOURTEEN-YEAR-OLD IN LOVE WITH LOVE!!

FINALLY SPRING CAME ANEW!!
きょろきょろ
KYORU
KYORU (GLANCE)

HARU-DORI-SAN!
MEME-CHAN! HOW HAVE YOU BEEN?
PACHI (SMACK)
GOOD!!
YOUR HAIR'S GROWN OUT.
SO HAS YOURS, HARU-DORI-SAN.
STOP CALLING ME HARUDORI.
I'M SORRY, TSUGUMI-CHAN!!
チヨ チヨ チヨ
GOOD-NESS.
FLIRTING LIKE THAT, RIGHT OUT IN PUBLIC.

SFX: CHIYO (CHIRP) CHIYO CHIYO

ぷぷんす
PUPUNSU
CHARRUMPH
ぷんす
PUNSU
ANYA-SAN!!
IT'S SO NICE TO SEE YOU AGAIN.
CAN'T YOU BE MORE GROWN-UP?
WE'RE FINALLY BACK TO-GETHER.
NOW THE TRIO GETS TO START OVER FRESH!!
LET'S DO OUR BEST!!
3
III
参

Y-YEAH, TOTALLY...
?
IS SOME-THING WRONG?
EXCUSE ME...
YES?
TEKE (TROT)
テケ
TEKE
テケ

I'M AO HOSHINO.
PEKKOSU (BOW)
I'M SKILLED IN USING THE "SCYTHE" PART OF THE HALBERD. NICE TO MEET YOU.☆
ANYA HEPBURN. I'M SKILLED AT THE "SPEAR" PORTION.
MEME TATANE... THE "AXE" PART...
TSUGUMI-CHAN'S TOLD ME SO MUCH ABOUT YOU TWO! I'M SO VERY HONORED TO FINALLY MEET YOU. ☆

SHIRA (STARE)
しら～
AOCCHI HELPED ME PRACTICE WHILE YOU TWO WERE GONE, AND, UM...
SHIRA
しら～
I HEAR YOU'RE BOTH FANTASTIC MEISTERS, SO I'M REALLY LOOKING FORWARD TO LEARNING A LOT FROM YOUR EXAMPLE.
TSU-GUMI
-CHAN!!
-SAN!!
YES...?

WHAT ARE YOU THINKING, TSUGUMI-SAN!!?
YOU'RE SUCH A PLAYER, TSUGUMI-CHAN!!
GAGANTOSU (GAGONG)
THIS IS MY SAVAGE BUT SUPER-FUN LIFE!

SOUL EATER NOT! 5 END

SOUL EATER NOT!

ATSUSHIYA
NOT! LOCATION

TITLE DESIGNED BY: ノ=Mamoru Miyano あ=Mamoru Miyano ッ=Haruka Chisuga つ=Haruka Chisuga ト=Kaori Nazuka し=Kaori Nazuka 支=Chiaki Omigawa 屋=Chiaki Omigawa 店=Dir. Masakazu Hashimoto

THANKS FOR VISITING US AT THE VERY, VERY END.
THIS IS THE END OF SOUL EATER NOT! AND THE SOUL EATER SAGA.
C'MON, GREET OUR GUEST...
......
......
WHAT'S WRONG?
I'M JUST GLAD YOU DIDN'T DECIDE TO END THE SERIES BY DRAWING IT WITH YOUR ASS.
WHAT?
OH, YOU MEAN THE TITLE UP THERE? HEY, IT'S A BETTER LINEUP THAN MY ASS, RIGHT?
THIS IS TERRIBLE... THEY DID YOU THE HONOR OF DRAWING YOUR TITLE CARD, AND YOU'RE TALKING ABOUT YOUR ASS! TAKE THAT BACK!!
WHAT? I DIDN'T ASK 'EM TO!
LIAR!! YOU CAME TO THEM HAT IN HAND ASKING FOR THEIR HELP, AND YOU WERE REAL EXCITED ABOUT IT! JUST ADMIT IT!!
GAAA (RAWR)
GAAA

OH, WHATEVER. WE GOT A NICE TITLE DRAWING THAT SUITS THE FINALE OF THE SERIES.
ALL I NEED TO DO IS SAY A BUNCH OF NICE CRAP, AND PEOPLE WILL EAT IT UP.
I FEEL LIKE YOU'RE NOT TAKING THIS SERIOUSLY.
SIGH...
YOU CAN HATE ME, BUT PLEASE DON'T HATE SOUL EATER.
SHIRAA (BABBLE)
THAT'S AN OLD LINE...AND IT DOESN'T WORK FOR YOU AT ALL.
"SOUL EATER" IS FOREVER IMMORTAL!!
DON (BOOM)
THAT'S NICE, BUT IT'S EVEN OLDER...
I JUST WANT TO BE AN ORDINARY GIRL AGAIN!!
OPPEKEPEPE (SHA-LALA)
THAT DOESN'T EVEN MAKE SENSE...
I'VE HAD ENOUGH OF YOU.
I'VE REACHED THE LIMIT OF MY STAMINA!
GUGUGU (STRAIN)
ALL RIGHT, WE'RE SHUTTING THIS DOWN.
ATSUSHIYA IS NOW CLOSED.
GATAN (CLUNK)

SIGN: ATSUSHIYA THE END

Translation Notes

Common Honorifics

no honorific: Indicates familiarity or closeness; if used without permission or reason, addressing someone in this manner would constitute an insult.

-san: The Japanese equivalent of Mr./Mrs./Miss. If a situation calls for politeness, this is the fail-safe honorific.

-sama: Conveys great respect; may also indicate that the social status of the speaker is lower than that of the addressee.

-kun: Used most often when referring to boys, this indicates affection or familiarity. Occasionally used by older men among their peers, but it may also be used by anyone referring to a person of lower standing.

-chan: An affectionate honorific indicating familiarity used mostly in reference to girls; also used in reference to cute persons or animals of either gender.

-senpai: A suffix used to address upperclassmen or more experienced coworkers.

-sensei: A respectful term for teachers, artists, or high-level professionals.

Page 48
Yngling: The Ynglings were a Scandanavian dynasty descended from the Norse god Freyr. Although early Yngling kings were likely mythological, later kings of the line may actually have ruled parts of Sweden and, later, Norway. One early text that references the Ynglings is the Old English poem, *Beowulf*, written as early as 800 BCE.

Page 137
Funes: A reference to the short story, *Funes el Memorioso* ("Funes the Memorious"), by Argentinean magical realist writer Jorge Luis Borges. Funes is a boy who hits his head falling off a horse and from that point on has perfect memory.

Page 209
"You can hate me, but...": A parody of a line uttered by idol singer Atsuko Maeda, who was the lead face of mega-hit idol group AKB48 for several years. When she announced that she was graduating from the group to pursue a solo career in 2012, she closed her announcement with the line, "You can hate me, but please don't hate AKB."

Forever immortal: A famous line from the retirement speech of legendary baseball player Shigeo Nagashima, a lifetime member of the Yomiuri Giants, Japan's most successful and prestigious team. During his seventeen-year career, the Giants were league champions eleven times. When he retired, he finished his speech with, "My Giants are forever immortal!"

Ordinary girl: The sign-off line of the pop idol group Candies in the 1970s. They famously announced their break up at the very height of their popularity, claiming they "just want to return to being ordinary girls again." That line spread like wildfire and became a catchphrase.

Limit of my stamina: A line from the retirement statement of Chiyonofuji, one of the most successful sumo wrestlers in history. Throughout his career, he was lighter and more compact than most of the top wrestlers, which earned him the nickname "The Little Yokozuna."

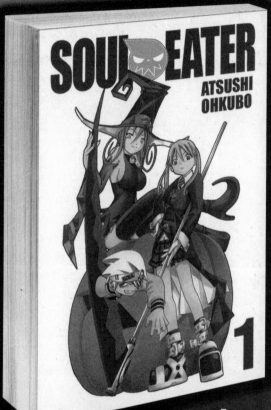

THE DEBUT SERIES FROM
ATSUSHI OHKUBO,
CREATOR OF
SOUL EATER
B. ICHI
B. ICHI
ATSUSHI OHKUBO
THE POWER TO SOAR LIKE A BIRD
OR FIGHT LIKE A TIGER:
ALL IT TAKES IS A HANDFUL
OF BONES.
Yen Press
Complete Volumes 1-4
AVAILABLE NOW!
OLDER TEEN
OT

The Phantomhive family has a butler who's almost too good to be true...
...or maybe he's just too good to be human.
Black Butler
YANA TOBOSO
VOLUMES 1-19 IN STORES NOW!
Yen Press
w.yenpress.com
BLACK BUTLER © Yana Toboso / SQUARE ENIX
Yen Press is an imprint of Hachette Book Group.
OLDER TEEN
OT

THE POWER TO RULE THE HIDDEN WORLD OF SHINOBI...
THE POWER COVETED BY EVERY NINJA CLAN...
...LIES WITHIN THE MOST APATHETIC, DISINTERESTED VESSEL IMAGINABLE.
Nabari No Ou
Yuhki Kamatani
COMPLETE SERIES NOW AVAILABLE
OLDER TEEN OT
Yen Press
Nabari No Ou © Yuhki Kamatani / SQUARE ENIX

DEALING WITH THE DEAD IS EVEN
WORSE THAN DEALING WITH THE DEVIL!
ZOMBIE-LOAN
BY PEACH-PIT
ZOMBIE-LOAN
PEACH-PIT
AVAILABLE NOW.
www.yenpress.com
Yen Press
OLDER TEEN
OT
ZOMBIE-LOAN © PEACH-PIT/SQUARE ENIX
Yen Press is an imprint of Hachette Book Group USA

MAXIMUM RIDE
LIKE YOU'VE NEVER SEEN HER BEFORE
VOLUMES 1-8 ON SALE NOW.
JAMES PATTERSON
MAXIMUM RIDE
8 NARAE LEE
Maximum Ride: The Manga © James Patterson
Illustrations © Hachette Book Group
Yen Press
w.yenpress.com
THE NEW MANGA SERIES BY
JAMES PATTERSON & NARAE LEE

THE NEW YORK TIMES BESTSELLING SERIES
Nightschool
WHERE DO DEMONS GET THEIR DIPLOMAS?
Schools may lock up for the night, but class is in session for an entirely different set of students. In the Nightschool, vampires, werewolves, and weirns (a particular breed of witches) learn the fundamentals of everything from calculus to spell casting. Alex is a young weirn whose education has always been handled through homeschooling, but circumstances seem to be drawing her closer to the nightschool. Will Alex manage to weather the dark forces gathering?
FROM SVETLANA CHMAKOVA, THE ARTIST OF WITCH & WIZARD AND CREATOR OF DRAMACON!
VOLUMES 1-4 AVAILABLE NOW
Nightschool © Svetlana Chmakova
Yen Press

R NOT! 5

ATSUSHI OHKUBO

Translation: Stephen Paul

Lettering: Abigail Blackman

Yen Press
Hachette Book Group
1290 Avenue of the Americas
New York, NY 10104

www.HachetteBookGroup.com
www.YenPress.com

Yen Press is an imprint of Hachette Book Group, Inc. The Yen Press name and logo are trademarks of Hachette Book Group, Inc.

The publisher is not responsible for websites (or their content) that are not owned by the publisher.

First Yen Press Edition: July 2015

ISBN: 978-0-316-30502-0

10 9 8 7 6 5 4 3 2 1

BVG

Printed in the United States of America